THE FIFTY-ONE PERCENT PRINCIPLE

PRINCIPLE

Taking Control Over Your Response to Life

UPCOMING BOOKS
BY WILLIAM C. LANTZ, JR.

Goal Therapy

Influence Therapy

The Unearned Relationship:
Relationship Therapy

THE FIFTY-ONE PERCENT PRINCIPLE

PRINCIPLE

Taking Control Over Your Response to Life

by
William C. Lantz, Jr., Ph.D.
and
Connie S. Lantz

Tulsa, Oklahoma

THE FIFTY-ONE PERCENT PRINCIPLE:
Taking Control Over Your Response to Life
ISBN 1-56292-104-5
Copyright © 1994 by William C. Lantz, Jr., Ph.D.
1127 S. Boulder
Tulsa, Oklahoma 74119

Published by Honor Books
P.O. Box 55388
Tulsa, Oklahoma 74155

ACKNOWLEDGMENTS
AND DEDICATION

When I was on the American Inter-Varsity staff after World War II, I had the privilege of spending many hours with Corrie ten Boom. It was with her that I was first faced with the fact that I had the primary and ultimate Responsibleness and Accountableness for my inner responses in spite of outer, tangible realities. If anyone knew about such things, it had to be Corrie ten Boom. After all, she had learned and lived them for years in a German concentration camp.

However, because I was not ready at the time to accept the concept of full Accountableness, I really didn't hear it. The fact is that I found it personally threatening. To me it seemed difficult, if not impossible, for anyone to handle such awesome responsibility. As time went by, I simply chose not to think much more about it.

However, over the years God kept bringing it back to me. While I was a professor at Fuller Seminary in California, I had an opportunity to spend hours with Victor Frankl when he visited the campus to share his principle of Logotherapy, which he had also put together while in a German prison camp. Still the concept of assuming personal responsibility and accountability for inner reactions despite outer realities did not totally "gel" for me.

Finally, when I heard Accountableness explained by James Newman (more about this subject in the Introduction), it all came together through four days of intense personal struggle with him and it.

I then fully accepted Accountableness even though it still seemed somewhat threatening to me. The threat subsided when I remembered what Corrie ten Boom had learned: to handle accountability takes God's empowering grace, a sense of oneness with Christ and the enabling power of the indwelling Holy Spirit.

I began to appreciate the hours I had spent personally with others who had taught me about God's power: Dawson Trotman, founder of the Navigators (I was one of several "Timothys" to his "Paul"); Stacey Woods, founder of American Inter-Varsity (he was my boss while I was there); Jim Rayburn, founder of Young Life (I once taught at the Young Life Institute); Bill Bright, founder of Campus Crusade for Christ (Bill and I were classmates at Fuller Seminary); and Oral Roberts (whom I got to know while teaching some classes at ORU). All these men reinforced the awareness that God's empowering grace was necessary in order to handle personal emotions.

With this knowledge, I had acquired the second half of the Accountableness/Responsibleness Theory — God's power to handle it. Armed with that fact, I fully accepted Accountableness, after years of trying to avoid it.

Others are included among those who taught me God's empowering, which enabled me to accept Accountableness and to write this book: Homer Goddard, my first Sunday School teacher, who led me to Christ; Bob Munger, whose influence was a big part of my call to the ministry; Louis Evans, my pastor during some of those early years; Dock Halverson, whom I knew in youth conferences when he was a pastor in California before becoming a U.S. Senate chaplain; Henrietta Mears, my later Sunday School teacher; Harry Ironside, who helped me write a term paper in college; Art Linkletter, who encouraged me in my move back to Tulsa; Wilbur Smith, who guided me to Fuller Seminary; Harold John Ockenga, Carl Henry, Ed Carnell and Charles Fuller, colleagues at Fuller Seminary; Jenkin Lloyd Jones, whose editorials in the *Tulsa Tribune* were the clearest articulation of Accountableness; Dr. L. D. Thomas and Dr. James Buskirk, my pastors in later years, who represent the epitome of encouragers, and who believed in me as I developed and taught Accountableness at First United Methodist Church of Tulsa; and my father, Bill Lantz, Sr., who taught at Tulsa Central High School for thirty-eight years and founded Kanakuk Kamp (even at my age, I am still known in Tulsa as Bill Lantz's son).

Above all, my wife, Connie Lantz, co-author of this book, needs to be recognized. Every thought and phrase in this work is something we have discussed together, counseled others about, taught together in class, communicated to our six children and nine grandchildren, prayed about together and in some cases wept over together. I doubt if any couple has been more in tune on a subject than we have on this one. Once I was trying to explain to someone how Connie and I felt about some of these ideas. I said, "Well, in the back of our mind . . ." The listener laughed and interrupted, "Do you have only one mind?" And it struck me that it was so.

As I thought over these acknowledgments and this dedication, I was astounded at the number of wonderful people God has allowed me to have contact with and the tremendous part they have played in the preparation of this presentation. So it is to these people that I dedicate this work. Each one of them has had a pivotal influence in my thinking, my ministry and my life — and in the writing of this book.

CONTENTS

INTRODUCTION

"He makes me mad."

"She upsets me."

"They depress me."

"That makes me miserable."

I had heard statements like those for years and never contested them. I had said them myself.

I had been a Christian for years, had studied the Bible thoroughly, in fact had been to seminary and was ordained, had a Ph.D. and was a counselor. Yet I did not remember hearing any serious arguments against these statements.

Then in the fall of 1960, at La Jolla, California, I attended the PACE Seminar, created and taught by James W. "Jim" Newman. For the first time I heard these statements renounced as irresponsible.[1]

Accountableness

Jim taught a different system. It started with a person's primary Accountableness for those chemical reactions going on inside of him that we call emotions, or feelings or attitudes — and the behavior that results. Participants in the seminar were challenged not to attribute the ultimate responsibility to people and things from their past or present — no matter how much harder it was made for them by anybody or anything.

This proposal seemed ridiculous to me. It appeared obvious to me that feelings (and resulting actions) were controlled by heredity and/or environment. I could not remember hearing anything else in all of my studies. I did not remember seeing evidence of Jim's proposal anywhere in the Bible.

For the first three days of the seminar I felt confusion. The third afternoon was free for recreation. I took my Bible and went out on the beach, determined to find out what the Scriptures teach on this subject. Before I left the beach a few hours later, I could scarcely find a page of the Bible on which this Accountableness principle was not set forth.

I had long before committed myself to Christ and Christian service, but here was a new dimension within my faith. From that day to this, this concept of Accountableness and Responsibleness has been a basic foundation of my ministry and counseling. The defining and applying of this concept is the subject of this book.

Chapter 1
A DIFFERENT SYSTEM

One problem is that this Accountableness system is a Minority point of view and is in conflict with what most people believe, teach and practice. I suspect that like most readers you will respond, at first, as I did — you will see it as ridiculous. Therefore, would you consider a method we often propose to a counselee?

Most people who come to us for counseling or classes want us to fix up their system. They have discomforts, ill health, insecurities, spiritual confusion, unhappiness, tension, etc.

They want us to patch up their wounds, repair the damage, overcome the pains, but within their system. They admit that their system isn't working, but they are not quite ready to try a different one. Our challenge to them is, "Would you be *willing* to try a different system, *willing* at least to consider it, *willing* at the very least to discuss it?"

Sometimes a building can be repaired. Sometimes it cannot be repaired. When it can't be, then no matter how it is fixed up, it is still going to be an inferior building.

So it is with a personal system — emotional, spiritual, behavioral, rational. Sometimes it can be fixed up. Sometimes it can't be. When it can't be, we frankly tell the counselee that we can't help him within his system.

If the counselee is willing to consider a different system, we usually make good progress. If he is not willing, we don't.

This challenge can be frightening to some people. We don't try to get them to change their mind. We ask them simply to *consider* a different system. They are usually at least willing to do that much. This is all we are asking of you in this book, that you consider a different system.

The Role-Playing Method

In difficult cases, I tell the counselee about an experience I had in college. As a sophomore on a state university campus, I was required, in my major, to take a year-long course in the great philosophers, starting with Aristotle. In those days, scientific skepticism was dominant on many public college campuses. Anything that could not be proved with the slide rule or the test tube was suspect. Religion had no place, and even the social sciences were on the defensive. Like many of my fellow students, I resented the requirement of the philosophy course.

The professor surprised us in the first class session by claiming to agree with scientific skepticism. He suggested, however, that one needs to consider timing. He said that if we start immediately with criticism of a system, we sometimes pick at surface items rather than get to the heart of the system.

He pointed out that every one of the philosophers we would study had a system. With a twinkle in his eye, he said he could show us how to rip each one apart, but from within the heart of the system. He had our attention.

He challenged us to consider each philosopher in two steps. In the first half we were to make sure we all understood the heart of that philosopher's system, by "role playing" a student of his, as if we were a follower of Aristotle, for example, back in the Lyceum in ancient Greece. The professor promised us that we would then spend an equal amount of time in the second half, criticizing the philosopher's system, but it would be judging the essence of the system, not peripheral matters. Then the same procedure would follow with each subsequent philosopher we studied.

We saw the professor as sincere. We agreed: 1) that any scientific approach that refuses to look at the alternatives is not truly scientific, 2) that temporarily acting as if we were a participant of a system did not make us more gullible and 3) that such role playing could help us know what to reject and why.

This approach appealed to us, and so we did the role playing. As a result, when we ultimately rejected a philosopher or any part of his system, we knew exactly why, with solid insight.

When we tell this story to a counselee, it often helps him to be more willing to look seriously at this different system. This is our challenge to you as a reader — that you take a look at this Accountableness system. If it differs from the system within which you have been operating, would you be willing to play the role of a participant in the system before you make a final decision?

What Is the System?

You may have wondered if this were just another book on emotions, feelings, attitudes! No, not really — it is a book on *Accountableness.*

People often agree on individual accountability in the area of behavior, but most people do not see accountability as applying equally to emotions: "Ya' can't help how ya' feel, for cryin' out loud!"

According to the Bible, we are just as accountable for inner emotions, feelings, attitudes, moods, spirit and "gut-level" experiences, as we are for overt actions, behavior, deeds and performances. In our study, we will look thoroughly at such Bible teachings.

Jesus condemned the Pharisees more than the Roman soldiers, the tax collectors or even the harlots. Why? Because, although they were extremely religious, their emphasis was upon only overt performance; they neglected the "heart," the inner being, the chemical reactions inside that we call emotions. (See Appendix C.)

A person can apparently be a Christian for some time and still see obedience to God only in behavior, not in emotions. He may not be aware of this principle even in the Bible. Once he sees emotions as an act of obedience (or disobedience) to God too, he never fails again to see it as basic in all Bible teachings.

Moral Content of Emotions

Why do people miss seeing Accountableness applied to emotions in all of Scripture? Some of the reasons are obvious. The first is the same as the Pharisees' problem just stated.

A second way of putting it is that they neglect the fact that emotions have *moral content*. Some people, even some Christians, state: "Emotions are not good or bad, it's what you do with them that counts." This philosophy was part of that position held by the Pharisees. Another way some state it is: "Feelings are neither right nor wrong, they just are." If this point is true, if emotions have no moral content, then the first point of Accountableness becomes academic, and the Bible becomes a book of half-truths.

Some emotions are always good: joy, peace, patience, kindness, gentleness, self-control, etc. — "the fruit of the Spirit" (Gal. 5:22).

Some emotions are always bad: vengefulness, bitterness, greed, lust, jealousy, hostility, rage, etc.

Some emotions can be either bad or good, depending on how much, how long, how often, in response to what, directed to what. An example is anger. The Bible tells us: "Be angry, and do not sin" (Ps. 4:4). "Be . . . slow to wrath" (James 1:19). "Do not let the sun go down on your wrath" (Eph. 4:26). Jesus was angry when He threw the moneychangers out of the temple, and when He criticized the Pharisees for their lack of compassion for others.

Other emotions that can be either good or bad are fear and sadness. Jesus was sad and cried at the death of Lazarus. (John 11:35.) He had fears, and sweat drops of blood when anticipating His betrayal and crucifixion. (Luke 22:41-44.) All of Jesus' emotions were right and appropriate. However, for us, fear can become excessive, even to the point of terror or panic. Sadness can become excessive to the point of depression and despair.

Can We Handle Accountability?

Jean-Paul Sartre, the leading Existentialist, did agree on the first two points — that we are accountable for our emotions and that they can be good or bad. However, he became a discouraged man. He saw that even though emotions have ethical content, and that we are accountable for them, we can't handle them![1]

And he was right. Which leads us to a third issue. Without God's help, we can't handle our emotions. It takes God's grace, His empowering and His enabling. "Without Me you can do nothing," Jesus said in John 15:5. Paul said, "I can do all things through Christ" (Phil. 4:13). It takes the power of the Holy Spirit, the indwelling Christ, to overcome emotions.

One reason this Minority concept of Accountableness for one's own emotions is so threatening to many people is because they are afraid they cannot handle that responsibility very well. And they are right, *without God they can't.*

Obedience in Emotions

The Christian who knows and takes his Bible seriously understands that he is commanded in Scripture to take charge of his emotions — to feel certain emotions and not to feel certain other emotions. To face and accept the fact of one's Accountableness for what is going on inside oneself is awesome! We will look in depth at emotions as an act of obedience, just as behavior, in Chapter 4.

This is a message that should be presented to everyone, Christian or non-Christian. When the non-Christian takes seriously this Accountableness, and realizes how impossible it is for him to handle it well, he may cry out for help. God has the help to give him, if he will take Christ into his life. (See Appendices A and B.)

The Responsibleness should not be so frightening to the Christian if he understands the power of the Holy Spirit in him, the presence of Jesus Christ within, the grace of God that enables him to handle this Accountableness increasingly well. God does not play games with us. If He commands us to feel certain emotions and to not feel certain others, then we know that by His grace it is possible.

Every command of God is an enabling.

So far, we have looked at four issues that we will consider in this book:

1. We are accountable for our emotions as well as for our behavior.

2. Emotions as well as behavior can have moral content.

3. With God's help, we can handle our emotions as well as our behavior — not instantly, easily or totally, but increasingly.

4. Emotions as well as behavior can be an act of obedience or disobedience to God.

Let us start our investigation of these issues with a written project that may help you sort them out and apply them personally. You will need a pencil.

Chapter 2
THE THREE OPTIONS

In the Introduction we saw that God commands us to feel certain emotions and not to feel certain emotions. We also saw that we are to help make changes in people, places, things, situations, circumstances — things outside of our skin — as well as the emotions inside of our skin. How do these two endeavors — our influence and our emotions — fit together?

To answer that question, let's do a simple personal evaluation together.

Analysis of the Problem

As a workshop project, pick *one person, place, thing or situation:*

That you do *not like,*

or

That you feel is putting *pressure* upon you,

or

To which you are responding with some kind of *tension.*

Now take your pencil, turn the page and identify the problem on the workshop sheet.

Identity of the Problem

The problem in my environment that is putting pressure upon me is:

Check only one: Name him, her, them or it:

(You can come back later   (Not yourself and not

and consider others, but   anything inside yourself

take one at a time.)   — something outside

yourself.)

_____A person: _____

         or

_____A place: _____

         or

_____A thing: _____

         or

_____A situation:_____

         or

_____An organization:_____

         or

_____A group:_____

         or

_____A law:_____

         or

_____Other: _____

Description of the Problem

Write below:

Some examples, a description or an explanation of how the person, place, thing, situation or pressure in your environment is *bad*:

_____

_____

_____

_____

_____

_____

_____

_____

_____

_____

_____

_____

_____

_____

_____

_____

_____

_____

_____

_____

Emotional Response to the Problem

Choose the best name for *your emotional feeling* (*inside* of you) in response to the problem or pressure: (Check one or more; limit yourself to three or four major ones.)

_____fretful irritation

_____anxious disharmony

_____frustrated discouragement

_____miserable distress

_____inner conflict of pressure

_____insecure worry

_____fearful apprehension

_____angry wrath, "mad"

_____sad depression

_____hostile rage

_____nervous tension or strain

_____disgruntled upset

_____"bugged," "uptight"

_____inner feelings of emptiness or bondage

_____excessive emotions of guilt and inferiority

_____hopeless spirit

_____hurt feelings, self-pity

_____"torn up," discord

_____covetous envy

_____ _____

(Other — write in)

Description of Emotional Response to Problem

Write below a sentence or two of *examples, description or explanation* of your *emotional feelings inside* your skin in response to the person, place, thing, situation or pressure outside. (Describe a little more in *detail* than just the word or words checked on the preceding page.)

_____

_____

_____

_____

_____

Examples:

I get so *irritated* around him, I lose my breakfast.

I feel so *miserable* about my situation, I want to yell.

I *hate* her and feel like *fighting.*

I get *depressed* and *worried* every time I go to the meeting.

I feel *inhibited* and all *choked up* to the point that I can't talk when I am in the office.

(Do not pick one of these samples; rather, write in the blank spaces above whatever way *you* really feel in response to the pressure that is on you.)

Possible Solutions to the Problem

OPTION I: *Influence* **the pressure or problem to change.**

Write below a sentence or two describing how the person, place, thing, situation or pressure *ought* to be (the way you would prefer if you could make the choice; what it would seem to take to enable you not to have the unpleasant emotions you have been feeling; the way you think God might want it to be; etc.):

_____

_____

_____

_____

Examples:

My wife be more *tolerant.*

My kids be *obedient.*

My boss be *open-minded.*

My church be *friendly.*

My neighborhood be more *neighborly.*

The police be more *helpful.*

Our laws be *consistent.*

(Do not pick one of these samples; rather, write in the blank space above whatever way you would really prefer *your* problem to be resolved.)

Evaluation of Option I

What is the *desirability* and *possibility,* with God's help, of your persuading, selling, demanding, requiring or in any way influencing the person, place, thing, situation or pressure to change, as stated on the preceding page?

A. _____ Possible and desirable

B. _____ Perhaps possible and desirable, perhaps not

C. _____ Impossible or undesirable

If you checked "C," then go back and put a big "X" across the preceding page, eliminating Option I.

OPTION II: *Physically avoid* the pressure or problem.

Write below a sentence or two describing the way or ways you could *withdraw from, get rid of, separate yourself from, escape from, eliminate*, put geographical space between yourself and the person, place, thing, situation or pressure. (Name one or more.)

_____

_____

_____

_____

Examples:

Get a divorce.	Have a nervous breakdown.
Quit the job.	Resign the office.
Leave town.	Leave the club.
Change churches.	Put the children up for adoption.
Fire the employee.	
Go on strike.	

(Do not pick from these samples; rather, write in the blank space above whatever way or ways you might really be able to escape *your* problem.)

Evaluation of Option II

What is the *desirability* and *possibility,* with God's help, of your dealing with the problem by escaping it as stated on the preceding page (possible and desirable, with *all* things considered, including whether it would be pleasing to God)?

A. _____ Desirable and possible

B. _____ Perhaps desirable and possible, perhaps not

C. _____ Undesirable or impossible

If you checked "C," then go back and put a big "X" across the preceding page, eliminating Option II.

OPTION III: *Change your inner emotions in spite of* the person, place, thing, situation or pressure.

Change what is going on *inside of you regardless* of what is taking place outside of you; change your emotions *anyhow, nevertheless.* (Check "A" or "B" below.)

A _____ I am *satisfied* with my emotions as stated on the check list and don't choose to change my emotions.
(I am satisfied because they feel comfortable, or help the other person or situation, or contribute to my physical health, or please God, etc.)

B. _____ I am *not satisfied* with my emotions as stated on the check list and would prefer to change my emotions if I could. (I am not satisfied because they do not feel comfortable, or don't help the other person or situation, or don't contribute to my physical health, or don't please God, etc.)

If you checked space "A," skip the next two pages.

If you checked space "B," see the next two pages.

Emotional Analysis

Things you cannot get from or give to others (i.e., emotions you have learned or may choose to unlearn or learn).

_____fretful irritation
_____anxious disharmony
_____frustrated discouragement
_____miserable distress
_____inner conflict of pressure
_____insecure worry
_____fearful apprehension
_____angry wrath, "mad"
_____sad depression
_____hostile rage
_____nervous tension or strain
_____disgruntled upset
_____"bugged," "uptight"
_____ inner feelings of
emptiness or bondage
_____excessive emotions of
guilt and inferiority
_____hopeless spirit
_____hurt feelings, self-pity
_____"torn up," discord
_____covetous envy

_____calm serenity
_____emotional stability and
strength
_____tranquil spirit
_____peace of mind
_____inner experience of
gladness and joy
_____good humor
_____emotion of
contentment
_____inner harmony and
composure
_____inner happiness
_____patience
_____relaxation
_____inner poise and
steadiness
_____emotional feeling of
fullness
_____emotional feeling of
inner freedom
_____empathic warm regard
_____enthusiastic zeal
_____good desires, tastes,
cravings

_____
(Other — write in)

_____
(Other — write in)

Evaluation of Option III

Write below a sentence or two about the *emotions* you would *prefer* to experience:

(Describe the emotions you would prefer to experience inside yourself from the right-hand column on the preceding page instead of those emotions in the left-hand column. Write a little more *detail* than just the word or words checked in the right-hand column.

_____

_____

_____

_____

Examples:

I would like to feel a little more *calm and emotionally stable* when I am around him, *no matter what* he does.

I would like to feel somewhat *content and confident, in spite of* the situation I find myself in at the moment.

I would like to have *patience and relaxation when* I am with her, *nevertheless.*

I would like to experience more *courage and optimism when* I go to the meeting, *however* it goes.

I would like to have a feeling of *release* and even feel *free* to be expressive *when* I am in the office, *whatever* happens.

I would like to have *peace of mind and inner joy, regardless* of how my employees vote.

I would like to have *inner harmony and tranquility, anyhow*, even when my son's wife doesn't treat my grandchildren properly.

(Do not pick one of these samples; rather, write in the blank spaces above whatever emotions *you* really would *prefer* to experience *regardless* of the problem.)

Review of the Three Options

_____ I. *Influence* the person, place, thing, situation, pressure to change.

_____ II. Physically *avoid* the person, place, thing, situation, pressure.

_____ III. Change my *emotions*. Not my emotions *about* it, but my emotions *in spite* of it. Not my opinions, evaluations, judgments, criticisms, points of view, beliefs, ideas about what is *outside* my skin — but my emotions *inside* my skin — *in spite of* the facts, *regardless* of the reality, *whatever* the truth — *anyhow, nevertheless* — especially when I cannot or should not influence the pressure to change (Option I) or cannot or should not avoid it (Option II).

CHOOSE FROM THE THREE OPTIONS and check in the space to the left. (Check one or more — but if you choose more than one, double check the major one.)

THERE IS NO FOURTH OPTION!

Review of Option I

Let's look carefully at each of the three options. Option I is sometimes right, possible and pleasing to God. The employer should influence his employees. The parent should influence his children. The teacher should influence his students. The Bible teaches that we are our brother's keeper and should be concerned to help others grow, progress, develop, increase and move ahead.

A problem is that Option I can be overdone, especially when it becomes an overbearing, pushing, whip-cracking, manipulative attempt to control. Within limits, it is in keeping with biblical standards to try to influence another person to change.

Since the other person owns 51% of his inner emotional feelings and responses, any influence we have never goes beyond 49%, never reaches the level of control; any attempt to go beyond our 49% is an attempt to control, and we don't have that ability. So in Option I, we are talking only about influence, not manipulation or control.

However, let's face it, sometimes even influence is not possible. Sometimes Option I is out altogether. Even when it is possible, there are limits. There is often an end to Option I.

Review of Option II

Option II is sometimes right. If the employer has done all he can to help the employee change (Option I), and the employee refuses, there is no reason why the employer should adapt himself to the employee (which would be Option III). It is sometimes right to fire the employee (Option II). But sometimes that is not practical because of laws, union rules, social factors, prior commitments, etc. So, sometimes Option II is out.

If your spouse is committing adultery and continuing to do so without repentance, this is the one biblical grounds for your getting a divorce (Option II). However, when we review Option III, we will see that the Bible talks as much about forgiveness as it does adultery, and as much about attitudes as actions.

If your church is teaching heresy, and you have done all that is possible to influence change, but the church refuses to alter its teaching, then Option II, leaving, is the biblical response.

If you have a court order not to leave town, it may be physically possible to do so anyway, but the consequences may make this Option II undesirable.

Do see that Option II is usually a possibility. Some people ignore Option II, even denounce it: "Don't ever run away from a problem; always face it head on." This is nonsense.

To be sure, it is wrong to overdo Option II, to *always* run away from *every* problem.

And, it is also wrong to *pretend* that you are not exercising Option II when you really are.

There is a time to put geographical space between yourself and the pressure, but sometimes it is not right, desirable or godly to do so. Sometimes it is not even possible, if you are in jail or in some other way being physically restrained.

Review of Option III

Now if the "bad news" is that Option I and Option II are sometimes both out, the good news is that Option III is always there as a last resort. This does not mean that Option III is better, but it is always possible.

Let's consider an example. An engineer came to see us for counseling because he had ulcers and was getting high blood pressure. I asked him if he knew of any pressure in his environment. He went into a several-minute tirade about the "ogre" who was his boss.

I asked if he felt there was any way that he could influence his boss to change (Option I). He answered that his boss would not even confer with him. I asked if a group from the department or the union could get his attention. He insisted that nothing was going to cause the boss to change. He thus agreed that Option I was out — that trying to influence the person or the situation to change was hopeless.

I challenged him to consider Option II. Why not quit the job? He objected that he had been with the company twenty-three years and would lose too many benefits by quitting. I suggested the possibility of transferring to a different department. He pointed out that his boss was head of engineering, and if he worked for that company it meant working under that boss. He thus agreed that Option II — avoiding the person or the situation — was also out.

I reminded him that the only option left was Option III — to change his own inner emotions in spite of the boss. He was offended and replied, "I don't think you understand the situation!" He started again with his tirade about the boss. I interrupted and insisted that I did agree with him about the boss, but Option III was the only one left. There is no fourth option. He objected, "But that's not fair!"

I agreed that it wasn't fair, but pointed out that God didn't promise us fairness. I reminded him that he had come in for help on his ulcers and high blood pressure, not on the issue of fairness.

When unfairness exists, we may sometimes be able to change the unfairness (Option I), but sometimes not. We may sometimes be able to avoid the unfairness (Option II), but sometimes not. But even when we cannot change (Option I) or avoid the unfairness (Option II), we can still keep our own inner harmony in spite of the unfairness (Option III).

I frankly told him that I could not help him with the unfairness, but that I could help him with the ulcers and high blood pressure. One might think of this book as counsel on how to avoid getting ulcers and high blood pressure, or to get rid of them, not as a list of ways to change unfairness when it is impossible to do so.

Option III Is Not: Hide Your Eyes, Grit Your Teeth or Knuckle Under

The engineer said somewhat defensively, "Well, you think I should *ignore* what he does, pretend that it's not really true, *hide my eyes* and play like everything is fine?" He thought this was what I was advocating.

I pointed out that such an attitude would not help his ulcers and high blood pressure.

Even more defensively, he countered, "Then I should just *grit my teeth*, and grin and bear it."

I insisted, "That will make your ulcers and high blood pressure worse."

He was at the end of his rope: "Am I supposed to just *knuckle under*, and let him run all over me?"

I suggested, "That's an interesting phrase — 'knuckle under.' In a way that's what you've been doing, letting him give you ulcers and high blood pressure — I would call that a form of knuckling under."

Totally exhausted, he exclaimed, "What do you want me to do?" I asked whether any of the other employees working under that boss were getting ulcers and high blood pressure. He replied no. I asked him how the others handled the boss' behavior. He had never thought about it before.

He thought out loud: "There's Ralph. Ralph has a terrific sense of humor. He laughs about it — not while the boss is there — but after the boss has thrown one of his tantrums, Ralph doubles up and exclaims, 'What a character!'

"Then there's George. George is a serious Christian. Everybody likes George. I think George feels sorry for him. I've heard George say more than once, 'There is a miserable human being.'"

The engineer had his "Aha!" He finally asked the right question: "Do you think I can really change my own inner emotions, even if the boss doesn't change?" He was ready now to understand the Accountableness principle. He began to see that he really did have the majority ownership of his own emotions and that he could increasingly by God's grace learn to change those emotions — not easily, not instantly, not perfectly, but he was willing to start learning and growing. He was ready to learn the tools that we discuss in our book *Goal Therapy*.[1] It took about six months, but he did get over his ulcers and high blood pressure.

Looking for Option IV

A person who is close to a breakdown and comes to see us for counseling is often saying: "Please help me find a fourth option!" This can be a part of mental illness — looking for a fourth option. And a part of mental health is willingness to work within the three options, even when it is not fair.

Fairness is not what produces mental health. What produces mental health is learning to live with unfairness when it can't be changed or avoided. It isn't what happens to us that matters; it is how we react to what happens to us. John Milton said: "Blindness is not what's miserable. What's miserable is unwillingness to endure blindness."

Misunderstanding Option III

Option III confuses some people. Occasionally, a counselee will say about it: "Well, that's what I've been doing, and I'm tired of it." We know immediately that he does not yet understand Option III. He is thinking of Option III as either hiding his eyes, gritting his teeth or knuckling under. It is none of those three. It is *really changing inside*.

Most counselees we see do agree that human beings can change how they *act* or how they *talk*, but most have not even considered the possibility that people can really change their *inner feelings*, inner tastes, inner responses. It is not that they reject such a concept — it's just that it has never been comprehended, never been "programmed into the computer."

Think of all the aphorisms: you can't teach an old dog new tricks, you can't make a silk purse out of a sow's ear, you can't change human nature, the leopard can't change his spots, etc. The passage about the leopard is found in Jeremiah 13:23 in the Bible, and the point is that with God all things *are* possible.

In our counseling and training programs, we are dedicated to the proposition that *people can change* — not just their behavior but their emotions as well. If this is not true, a counseling career is hardly worthwhile.

When a person says, "I have been exercising Option III and am tired of it," he is saying, "I'm tired of being happy — I prefer to be miserable," or, "I'm tired of making myself happy. I want someone else to make me happy." My response to that attitude is: "Good luck!"

Another misconception is that Option III is a weak position, that if we choose it we will be less able to exercise Option I or II. Let's look at an example.

The Strength of Option III

In a group therapy session, one woman stated that her problem was that her little boy, Johnny, slammed the door, and that every time he did so she jumped three feet out of her chair and screamed at the top of her voice. We went through the Three Options. Her first point was that she did choose Option I — to influence Johnny to change.

Option II would entail something like putting the boy up for adoption. She refused even to consider it. Even though Option II sometimes seems ridiculous, we still encourage a counselee at least to consider it in order to know for sure *why* he is rejecting it. It is important that he see, under Option II, that the issue is not that he *can't* get a divorce, quit his job, leave the church, etc. *Not to* is a real choice, and he needs to understand why he chooses it — that it is not productive, godly, efficient, enjoyable, healthy, etc. "Can't" often is a denial of Accountableness. "Choose to" or "choose not to" is usually facing it.

When we got to Option III, for Johnny's mother to change her own emotions, she was defensive. She insisted that Johnny was *causing* her responses, that she did not have responsibility for them. She used a common "cop out": "That's just the way I am!"

I asked if she meant that she was born that way, and she replied affirmatively. I suggested that a baby does have an inborn response to flinch at a loud noise — but three feet high, and to scream at the top of her voice! She saw the humor and replied, "Well, maybe I added a little." When I asked her if she was willing to work on the "little" she had added, she argued that it wouldn't do any good.

I asked her why she thought Johnny slammed the door. She said, "I know why he does it — he does it to bug me."

"But he didn't know the first few times that it was going to bug you," I responded.

She replied that the first time or two it was probably because he was in a hurry: "Kids always seem to be in a hurry. He probably came running through and just gave it a fling. But I think after that he did it to bug me."

I suggested that she prayerfully work on her own emotions (not hiding her eyes, gritting her teeth or knuckling under), to *really, truly* change on the inside, by God's help, to the point that she could rise calmly from her chair and say in a firm but calm voice, "Johnny, come back and close the door properly. You know how gentlemen close doors." And I suggested that she insist that he do it, then say to him: "Now, Johnny, I want you to remember this new rule. Every time you slam the door within my hearing, you will come back and do it right."

She wasn't buying it: "Oh, he'll keep on slamming the door."

"You said one of the reasons he slams it is to bug you," I answered. "Now if you don't put on the song and dance anymore, you have taken away that motivation. You said the other reason was that he was in a hurry. Now it will take him longer to get where he's going when he slams it. He would be stupid not to wake up to the fact that the fastest way to get where he is going is to do it right the first time."

"Well, he's not stupid," she replied skeptically.

I said that I thought he would learn to close the door properly.

She still wasn't buying. She was defensive and added a brand new dimension: "Well, I have a right to get upset. When he slams the door, it wakes the baby!"

"Does your jumping and screaming help the baby get back to sleep?" I asked.

We lost her at this point.

She felt she had a right to get upset, that her emotions belonged to her and that she had a right to feel tension, anxiety, frustration, misery, uptightness, etc., if she chose. It was important that she see her emotions as chosen and learned, and that if God would be more pleased if she were to feel inner composure, stability, calmness, equilibrium, etc., then by God's grace she could learn to change her choice and unlearn at least part of her response.

Understanding Option III

When we say that her emotions were a choice, we admit also the role of emotions as response (suddenly and impulsively engendered) but later to be channeled and well controlled. In Chapter 4 on the Amazing Commands, we will see that it is not only positive emotions that come under command. When negative and self-preservation emotions (e.g., anger, fear, frustration, etc.) erupt, there is a sense in which, at that exact moment, one is helpless to respond otherwise. It is not at that point a conscious, deliberate, willful decision. However, a series of choices has led to such automatic reactions. For the most part, they have been learned over a period of time. How they will now be channeled, managed and better controlled is what we will examine further in the following chapters.

The ultimate point about Johnny's mother is that allowing her own emotions to get out of control was not helping her to train Johnny. If anything, keeping her own emotions under control would probably help her do a better job of training her son.

Changing one's emotions (Option III) may help in changing the situation (Option I) or in avoiding the situation (Option II). Changing the situation (Option I) or avoiding the situation (Option II) *does not help* in changing one's own emotions (Option III) — except on a temporary basis. We will deal more with these principles in the next chapters.

But be careful — by *changing* one's emotions we do not necessarily mean having *fewer* emotions or *quieter* emotions. There is a time and a place for *more* anger, more grief, and more concern, etc. (as we see in Jesus).

One final reminder — if you do *choose* not to exercise Option III, so be it. See it as a "choose not to," rather than a "can't." It does take time and energy to learn how to change your own inner emotions. Sometimes the situation is simply not worth the time and energy it takes to learn to make this change — but the fact remains that you can choose to do so if you really want to.

When we say that emotions are choices, we mean as compared to choices to play the piano, type on the typewriter or fly an airplane. All these choices mean cultivation over time with energetic discipline, practice, repetition, learning. We will be going further into choice *and* cultivation, selection *and* repetition, decision *and* discipline, making up your mind *and* then practicing over and over the action you have decided to take.

Sometimes it would be wrong to cultivate emotions of contentment and tranquility (Option III). If your company is being dishonest, if your city government is being corrupt, if your church is being heretical, and if Option I, to change the people or the situation, is not possible, then the right answer is possibly Option II, to depart, not Option III, to alter your responses. But when you do rule out Option III, make sure you see it as a choice, and not as an inability.

Remember: *Every command of God is an enabling.*

The final criterion as to when and how to use Option III, according to Scripture, is to see *emotions* as acts of obedience or disobedience to God, as much as you see *behavior* as acts of obedience or disobedience to God.

We will deal with *how to* change our emotions (Option III) in the following chapters. First we need to understand better the differences between the two theories — the Majority Theory that somebody or something controls our responses, or the Minority Theory that we control them ourselves.

Chapter 3
THE MAJORITY POINT OF VIEW AND THE MINORITY POINT OF VIEW

In Chapter 2 we saw that sometimes it is right and possible to influence the outside pressure so as to bring about its change (Option I).

We also saw that it is sometimes right and possible to put geographical space between ourselves and the pressure (Option II).

Some people see only those two options in dealing with the pressure — change it or avoid it.

When we make the suggestion, as we did in Chapter 2, about changing our own emotions *in spite of* the pressure (what we are now calling Option III), the majority of people do not see "changing our own emotions" as appropriate, do not believe it to be possible or do not even know what it means.

The Majority Point of View

Most people in our society believe that emotions are *caused*.[1]

This Majority Point of View is that emotions are:

products	offshoots
consequences	effects

outcomes   etc.

results

Emotions are thus seen as the result of *action and reaction*. Included in this definition of what we are calling emotions are:

feelings	inner responses
attitudes	motivations
inner "gut-level" experiences	tastes
inner mood	desires
inner spirit	etc.

We are talking about *body chemistry* responses, the intensity of which we can scientifically measure with biofeedback instruments in the laboratory.[2,3]

Specifically, the following list is an alphabetical catalog of examples of such emotional feelings.

Terms Used to Identify Emotional Feelings (Measurable by Body Chemistry)

AFFECTION
ANGER
ANXIETY feelings
APPREHENSIVE emotions

BEWILDERED
BITTERNESS
"BLUE"
BONDAGE emotional feelings
BOTHERED

CALMNESS
CARING feelings
CHEERFULNESS, no matter what
inner CONFLICT, "TORN" emotions
emotion of CONTENTMENT, whatever
COMPOSURE
CORDIALITY feelings
COURAGEOUS emotions
COVETOUSNESS

DEFENSIVE emotional feelings
inner emotional feelings of DEJECTION
DELIGHT
DEPRESSIVENESS
DESIRE, CRAVINGS, TASTES
DISCORD in emotions
DISCOURAGED feelings
DISGRUNTLED
DISHARMONY in emotions
inner emotional feelings of DISTRESS
"DOWN" feelings

EAGERNESS
ECSTATIC
ELATION
inner feelings of EMPTINESS
ENRAGED
ENTHUSIASM

emotional feelings of FULLNESS
FERVOR

FORLORN feelings
feeling FREE
FRETFULNESS
FRIENDLY emotional feelings
FURIOUS
emotions of FRUSTRATION
inner emotions of FUTILITY
FURY

GLAD feelings, regardless
GLOOMY
GUILTY feelings
"GUSTO"

inner HARMONY of emotions
feelings of HAPPINESS, anyhow
inner emotional feelings of HOPELESSNESS
HOSTILITY
good HUMOR, nevertheless
HURT feelings

inner emotional feelings of INFERIORITY
INFURIATED
inner emotional feeling of INSECURITY

JOY, in spite of things

LIVELINESS feelings
"LOCKED-IN" inner feelings
"LONGSUFFERING" (patience in hardship)
LOST feelings

LOVING emotions
LUST

"MAD"
MELANCHOLY
emotional MISERY
MOROSE

"NERVES"

OUTGOING spirit

PANIC
PATIENT spirit
PEACE of mind
feelings of PLEASURE
inner POISE
POSITIVE mood
inner PRESSURE feelings

RAGE
RESENTFUL emotions

SAD
emotionally SECURE feelings
SERENITY
"SORE"
emotional STABILITY
feelings of emotional STEADINESS
inner emotion of STRAIN
emotional STRENGTH

TRANQUIL feelings
TERRIFIED
feeling THREATENED
"TORN-UP" feelings
TROUBLED emotions

"UPSET" feelings
"UPTIGHT"

VICIOUS feelings
VINDICTIVENESS feelings

So the Majority believe that these emotions are *caused* — by what? By:

> heredity
>
> parents
>
> environment
>
> body conditions
>
> events
>
> circumstances
>
> biology
>
> situations
>
> happenings
>
> etc.

The Majority assumes that emotional feelings are *produced* by *something.* When I state this Majority Point of View, people who are within that Majority are often surprised. They exclaim, "Majority! What do you mean Majority? What other point of view could there possibly be? Of course emotions are caused. Anybody knows that.

You can't help how you feel. Our backgrounds produce our emotions — our heredity and/or environment, nature and/or nurture, genetics and/or conditioning. There *couldn't* possibly be any other point of view."

Not so! There is a Minority viewpoint. That view is that emotions are *chosen* and *learned* — they are:

> decisions
>
> acts of the will
>
> a making up of one's mind
>
> picked out
>
> committed to
>
> selected
>
> etc.

and *then learned* through:

> repetition
>
> practice
>
> cultivation
>
> discipline
>
> drill
>
> etc.

If this Minority Theory seems ridiculous to the Majority, it is partly because both the selection and the repetition can be *subconscious;* in fact, they usually *are* subconscious.

Choice: An Instantaneous Reaction Compared With a Process (Majority Argument Number 1)

The Majority person typically brings up *three main arguments.*

First, he asks, "How can emotions be a choice?[4] If I'm feeling *sad* or depressed, I can't just snap my fingers and instantly choose to feel *cheerful* or happy!

"If I'm *angry* or hostile, I can't just snap my fingers and immediately choose to feel *calm*, composed or loving.

"If I'm feeling *fearful* or anxious, I can't just snap my fingers and quickly choose to feel *confident* and relaxed."

These statements are true. But they are true of *most choices*. Choice is seldom an instant, snap-your-fingers kind of action.

Choice in Physical Behavior

If one *chooses* to play the piano, he doesn't just snap his fingers and expect immediately to play. He takes piano lessons and practices.

If a person *decides* to type on the typewriter, he doesn't expect to sit down, then and there, and be able to type a letter. He knows that he will have to sign up for a typing class first and cultivate the skill through drill and repetition.

If someone *makes up his mind* to fly an airplane, he doesn't pick up the ignition keys, climb into the plane and try hard to take off. He signs up for flight training and goes through the discipline of learning how to fly, by going over the information and practicing the skills again and again.

Choice of change in such *physical behavior* implies that the decision is followed by implementation of that selection through some kind of repetition, the same way the person learned his old behavior.

Choice in Emotional Responses

In the same way as these choices of change in overt behavior, choice of change in *emotions* also implies that the decision is followed by implementation of that selection through some kind of repetition. This choice and repetition is the way the person learned his old emotions, even though that original learning may have been subconscious. The *confusion* in the mind of the Majority often comes from their forgetting that choosing and learning can be *subconscious*. First let's look at a behavior pattern and then an emotional pattern.

When little toddler, Johnny, spits out the oatmeal, his choice may not be a conscious one — but it can still be a choice. That is, he could choose to swallow it, or he could choose to spit it out. He does not make the choice to swallow it — which is a choice to spit it out.

First of all, we are not criticizing Johnny for his decision if he is not *consciously* aware that he is making a *choice.*

Second, even later, when Johnny becomes aware that he *is* making a choice — a conscious, deliberate, willful selection — to spit out the oatmeal, we are still not necessarily criticizing him; he does not yet know that his choice is a *bad choice.* He doesn't yet understand how good oatmeal is for him. He has not yet learned about proteins, vitamins and minerals. If he does not have the information necessary to motivate him to change his original choice, we are still not inclined to censure him.

Third, unless there is some reason for changing his choice, it becomes a *habit pattern* through repetition over a period of time. By the time he learns that not eating oatmeal is a bad choice, it may have become a habit. So we are still not blaming him even as an adult for the habit of disliking oatmeal — it has simply become automatic over time, through repetition.

However, we have some good news for Johnny. *It is not too late!* He can learn to change his choices, his tastes, his feelings, his behavior. He may not be able to change instantly, or easily, or totally — but he can change significantly and increasingly.

Emotions and tastes are mostly learned. And what has been learned can usually be unlearned. One can learn to smoke, and one can learn not to smoke. One can learn to feel sad, but one can unlearn sadness and learn cheerfulness. Learning and unlearning are essentially the same two-pronged process: 1) selection, or choice, or decision — even though such "making up one's mind" can be subconscious — and 2) repetition, practice, cultivation — even though that "self-discipline" can also be subconscious.

Choosing and Learning Applied to Emotions

Little Jimmy's mother refuses to give him candy. Jimmy has tried everything he can think of to get what he wants, but to no avail. Finally, he tries something new and different. He has heard of this, or seen it, or maybe he just thought it up. Jimmy lies on his back on the floor, kicks his heels against the floor and screams at the top of his voice.

If this happens to be in the middle of the first floor of the town's leading department store, Mommy might give in — "Okay, Jimmy, shut up, I'll give you the candy." Aha! It worked this time, and therefore he may try it again sometime.

However, we are not criticizing Jimmy for making this choice if he is not aware that it is a choice, if it is *not a conscious choice*. It just feels right to him.

Even when Jimmy begins to realize that he is making a choice, we are still not necessarily condemning him if he does not yet understand that it is a *bad choice*.

By the time he realizes that it is a bad choice, it may have now, through repetition, become an automatic, natural, free-flowing, spontaneous, genuine *habit pattern*. So we are not necessarily even then blaming him. In a sense, at a given moment he may be truly helpless to behave other than in accord with his habit pattern. But it is *not too late!* With God's help, Jimmy can unlearn in exactly the same way he learned — by selection and repetition. He can choose to change.

We are now adding a *fifth issue* to the original four. We might summarize the four as *accountability, morality, empowering* and *obedience.* Now comes the *fifth: process* — the procedural nature of choosing and learning emotions.

The point of reviewing and adding this fifth concept is to relate all of them to the first major argument of the Majority based on the assumption that choice of emotions implies merely instantaneous decision.

When the Majority Theory person sees choice as a part of *learning,* and not necessarily as an *instantaneous* or even *conscious* choice, he sometimes retracts his first argument. He may face and accept the fact of his own Accountableness for his own emotions since they are chosen and learned. But he still has two more objections.

"Cause and Prevent" Compared With "Harder and Easier" (Majority Argument Number 2)

The Majority person moves to his next major argument: "Don't you think that *heredity, parents, background, environment,* etc., have *anything* to do with behavior and emotions?"[5] The answer is, *of course,* they have *plenty* to do with them. Let's start first with behavior.

It apparently is *harder* for one person to control his *alcohol* intake than for another. Some people feel that this difficulty may be a chemical, inborn, allergy-type weakness. Or they feel that the early environment made it *easier* for the person to drink and become alcoholic. *But* this debate between heredity and conditioning is academic and irrelevant. The Bible commands us not to be drunken *nevertheless* (Eph. 5:18), even though it may be *harder* for one of us and *easier* for another.

It is *more difficult* for one person to control his *weight* than another. There are real differences in metabolism, thyroid functioning, early conditioning, etc., which can make it *harder* for one person to lose weight than another. *But,* spending much time debating this difference tends to evade the real issue. The Bible still commands us to keep our bodies under subjection (1 Cor. 9:27), *in spite of* the fact that it is *harder* for one person and *easier* for another.

It may be *harder* for one person to resist the temptation of *homosexuality.* Some people think that it is inborn, hormonal differences that make this problem *harder* for one than for another. Others argue that what makes it *harder* for one and *easier* for another is background, upbringing and other environmental factors. Arguing either way, heredity or environment, or both, can be a "cop out." The Bible commands us not to be homosexual *anyhow* (Rom. 1:27), even if it is *harder* for one and *easier* for another.

The debates, which tend to go on and on, as to whether these behaviors are a result of heredity or environment, are a "red herring," a way of avoiding dealing with the third factor of choice and accountability. The vigor and persistence with which the Majority limits the debate to only the two factors may prove their determination not to face Responsibleness. A classic example is a basic psychology textbook by Munn, Fernald, and Fernald.[6] In Chapter 2 the authors spend twenty-eight pages debating environment versus heredity, nature versus nurture, etc., without any mention of choice or Responsibleness as a third factor — as though it didn't exist, from a scientific approach.

The point of the Accountableness Theory is not to be judgmental about anyone's behavior or emotions. Let God do that if it needs to be done. It is saying that it is not too late for a person to change his choice.

Emotions as Well as Actions May Be Harder To Change

It is *harder* for one person and *easier* for another to control his *temper*. Parental upbringing, biology, present circumstances, etc., may make it *harder* or *easier*. However, the Bible commands us to control our temper *anyhow, even if* it is *harder* for one of us than for another.

It is *harder* for one person to be *cheerful* and easier for him to be *depressed*. And those background and circumstantial factors beyond his control may make it *harder* for him to be cheerful than for another. But the Bible commands us to be cheerful *anyway, even though* it is *harder* for one person than for another.

It is *harder* for one person not to be *fearful* and to be *confident*. What makes it *harder* may well be his genes and chromosomes, or parental history or present situation. The Bible commands us not to be fearful *regardless*, no matter how much *harder* it is for one than for another.

Yes, heredity, parental influence, past or current environment, etc., have a powerful influence upon our emotional feelings and attitudes. The most, however, that they can do, even all of them put together, is to make it *harder* or easier for one person to have certain emotions than it is for another person. They do not *control* our emotions — they do not *cause* some and *prevent* others.

If one refuses to make any place at all for the third factor of choice — in addition to the two of heredity and environment — then there is no meaning to accountability, responsibility, creativity, imagination, initiative, individuality, morality, values, etc.

The Majority often believe that the criminal is considered no longer accountable for his actions — they are simply the result of what society has done to him. The goofing-up employee is sometimes considered no longer accountable for his ineptness — the fault lies in what the capitalistic system has done to him. The flunking student may be considered no longer accountable for his failure — it is the result of what the school system has done to him. The misbehaving child is frequently considered no longer accountable for his behavior — it is the consequence of what the parents have done to him.

The other alternative, if the causes are not thus environmental, is that the causes of such responses are considered, by the Majority, to be hereditary. *Or,* some combination of heredity and environment is supposedly the cause.

If there is no third factor, which we call choice, then all of the responses are *caused* or *prevented,* without control by the individual. Some of those who initially side with this point of view of the Majority back down when they see the ultimate implications.

So we, in the Minority, *agree* with the Majority on the power of these other influences. But our Minority Point of View is that all they can do is make it *harder* for one person than for another, and the Bible commands certain emotional feelings and behaviors even so.

The Issue of Fairness
(The Third Argument of the Majority)

Even if the Majority person sees 1) the reality of choice as involving learning and process, rather than being instantaneous, and even if he sees 2) that choice and accountability do not minimize the power and importance of heredity, environment, etc., he usually still has a third and final objection.

The *third* and final argument that the Majority person sets forth is that the Minority Theory of Accountableness is *not fair*! "It is not fair for life to be *harder* for one person than for another. It is not fair for God to command us to feel certain emotions and not to feel certain emotions when it is so much harder for one person to do so than it is for another."

On this point, we agree — it's not fair. But who said that life is supposed to be fair? Some people get so stuck on this issue of fairness that they never get beyond it to the real, functional issues. Perhaps for some the fairness issue is a way of deliberately, or subconsciously, avoiding facing the real issues.

We now have added a sixth and seventh theme to the Minority Theory.

The Seven Themes

We have now touched on the seven basic themes to be developed in this book:

1) *Accountableness*

The primary and ultimate *accountableness* for our emotions as well as our behavior lies with us.

2) *Moral Content*

Emotions as well as behavior have *moral content* — some are always good, some are always bad, some can be good or bad, depending on several variables.

3) *God's Empowering*

By the *grace of God*, we have the capability of increasingly handling well that Accountableness for emotions as well as behavior.

4) *Obedience*

Since God's commands include emotions as well as behavior, emotions, like behavior, can be an act of *obedience* or disobedience to God.

5) *Choice and Learning*

Emotions, like behavior, are chosen and learned, but those selections and repetitions can be subconscious.

6) *Influence of Background*

Background factors — heredity and/or environment — can make it harder or easier for a person to choose and learn certain emotions, just as those background and situation factors can make it harder or easier for him to choose and learn certain behaviors. And that may not be fair.

7) *Priority of Emotions Over Behavior*

In the first six themes we have been simply indicating that each of the six applies equally to emotions as well as to behavior. The underlying implication goes further — emotions have *priority* over behavior. (See Appendix C.) The Pharisees not only missed the point — they revised it. We will now discuss this and all the other six themes.

Chapter 4
THOSE AMAZING COMMANDS IN THE BIBLE!

If I should ask you to raise your right hand, you could do it. If I should request you to tap your left foot on the floor three times, you could. But suppose I should order you: "Rejoice!" Would that be more difficult? Does it seem impossible to control voluntarily an *internal* experience such as joyfulness?

The Command To Rejoice

Yet, this command is given to us in the Bible! We are told to rejoice in all we put our hand to (Deut. 12:18), to rejoice and be exceedingly glad (Matt. 5:12), to rejoice with those who rejoice (Rom. 12:15), to rejoice always (Phil. 4:4), to rejoice evermore (1 Thess. 5:16 KJV), etc. These are imperatives, injunctions, orders, commands!

What Amazing Commands!

If the Bible had commanded us merely to perform some of the *actions* that are associated with joyfulness, we might control our muscles to produce such behavior. For example, if we were commanded to *smile*, we could do this as readily as we did the raising of the hand or the tapping of the foot. If the order were simply to hold our *heads high*, throw our *shoulders back* or put a *lilt in our voices*, we could obey. But the command deals with something deeper — *inner joy*. We are *commanded to rejoice*!

The Command To Desire

Another Amazing Command the Bible gives us is to *desire* the pure milk of the Word. (1 Pet. 2:2.) (See also Job 23:12; Psalm 1:2, 40:8; 119; Jeremiah 15:16; Colossians 3:16; James 1:18-21.) If the command had been merely to read, listen, memorize, discuss or make any other *overt* response to the Word, we could do it. But can we, by conscious, deliberate, willful response, control our reaction to God's Word in what could honestly be called a deep *desire*?

Not only toward the Scriptures is our desire commanded, but we are also commanded to desire spiritual gifts (1 Cor. 12:8,9; 14:1) such as wisdom, knowledge, faith, healing, etc. We are also commanded what not to desire — our neighbor's wife or his possessions. (Deut. 5:21.) Our desires are something we *are in charge* of and *accountable* for. We are responsible to *change* them when advisable. (See Psalm 37:4; Proverbs 23:3; Colossians 3:5.)

The Command To Love

Then there is that Amazing Command *to love* — love our neighbors, love the brethren, love our wives, love our husbands, even love our enemies. (See Leviticus 19:18; Deuteronomy 6:5; Luke 6:27; Ephesians 5:25; Colossians 3:14; Titus 2:4; 1 Peter 4:8 NIV; etc.)

If the command had been merely to exercise generosity, show kindness, express sympathy, be helpful, give praise or produce other physical *behavior* that might be considered a part of love, these activities could be performed if we worked hard enough. But love!

Is love something we can turn on and off like a faucet? Can I look at a person who is difficult for me to love and say, "I'm going to love him!" — and then grit my teeth and do it?

Other Commands About Emotions, Feelings or Attitudes

The Bible gives us other Strange and Amazing Commands. Let's review the three we have covered: rejoice, desire and love. Then let's look briefly at some of the others.

Amazing Commands

Rejoice

Deuteronomy 12:18
Matthew 5:12
Romans 12:15
Philippians 4:4
1 Thessalonians 5:16

Desire

Deuteronomy 5:21
Job 23:12
Psalm 1:2; 37:4; 40:8; 119
Jeremiah 15:16
1 Corinthians 14:1
Proverbs 23:3
Colossians 3:5,16
James 1:18-21
1 Peter 2:2

Love

Leviticus 19:18
Deuteronomy 6:5
Luke 6:27
Ephesians 5:25
Colossians 3:14
Titus 2:4
1 Peter 4:8 NIV

Set our *affection* . . . put to death inordinate affections —
Colossians 3:2,5 KJV

Not be *anxious* — Philippians 4:6

Stay *cool* when insulted — Proverbs 12:16

Be *compassionate* — Ephesians 4:32

Have *courage* — Psalm 31:24; 1 Corinthians 16:13

Be *enthusiastic* — Ecclesiastes 9:10; Romans 12:11

Hate *evil* — Romans 12:9

Fear not — Isaiah 41:10

Forgive — Ephesians 4:32; Colossians 3:13

Not be *greedy* for money — Titus 1:7

Be *humble* — Colossians 3:12; James 4:10

Not be *jealous* — Proverbs 27:3

Be *patient* — Luke 21:19; 1 Timothy 6:11; James 1:4-7

Have *peace* — Philippians 4:6,7; Colossians 3:15

Avoid *resentment* — 1 Timothy 2:8; Hebrews 12:14,15

Feel *sympathy* — 2 Corinthians 1:4; Philippians 2:1;
1 Peter 3:8

Control *temper, anger, wrath, rage, malice* — Psalm 37:8;
Proverbs 19:11; 16:24; Ecclesiastes 7:9;
Matthew 5:22; Ephesians 4:26; Colossians 3:8;
1 Timothy 2:8

Be *thankful* — Colossians 3:15; 1 Thessalonians 5:18

Not be *vengeful* — Romans 12:19

To some people it does not make sense to be commanded to control these inner attitudes, feelings and experiences.

Are They Really Commands?

Some people have tried to escape the force of these commands — commands to feel or not to feel certain emotions — by suggesting that the Bible does not really mean them. The orders are supposedly only ideals, or reminders, or concepts to believe in and teach about, or promises of what it will be like in heaven, or rules applicable to a different "dispensation," or illustrations to show us what we cannot do so that we will be more humble and trusting. Still the question may come back, "Suppose they really are commands?"

How To Obey the Command To Rejoice

If we feel a lack of *joy* in our life, we may be tempted to pray, "Lord, give me more joy." This prayer is not legitimate. As Christians, what is our source of joy? According to Jesus, "'These things I have spoken to you, that *My* joy may remain in you, and that your joy may be full'" (John 15:11 emphasis added). Ours is not just a joy like that of Christ — but the very joy of Jesus himself, personally in us. If you are a believer, then Christ lives in you. (See Appendix A.) Since He does personally live in you, then you do have His joy in you.

Jesus was a man of joy as well as a man of sorrows. We are told in the Scriptures that He had joy even in going to the cross. (Heb. 12:2.) Christ's joy in you better be enough — because that's all you're going to get. (See Appendix B.) And it is enough. (Phil. 4:19).

The Christian prayer then becomes, "Father, I thank You that Christ lives in me. I thank You that I have His joy in me. Forgive me for not being aware enough of it, for not appreciating it enough, for not expressing it enough, but I thank You that it is really here, because He is really here. Now, Lord, help me to get rid of whatever is keeping me from experiencing and showing forth that joy that I really do have in Christ."

How To Obey the Command To Have Peace of Mind

Do not pray, "Lord, give me more *peace of mind*." Jesus said, "'Peace I leave with you, *My* peace I give to you; not as the world gives do I give to you. Let not your heart be troubled, neither let it be afraid'" (John 14:27).

As Christians, we have a peace not merely *like* that of Christ. It is the very peace of Jesus himself, personally in us.

The Christian prayer becomes, "Lord, thank You that I have Christ's peace. Forgive me for not recognizing it and using it enough, but thank You that it is really here. Now help me to avoid anything that would prevent me from realizing and enjoying that peace that I really do have."

How To Obey the Command To Love

Think of a person it is difficult for you to *love*. Never pray, "O God, give me more love for Sally or Sam." The Scriptures tell us, "The love of God has been poured out in our hearts by the Holy Spirit who was given to us" (Rom. 5:5). Your body is the temple of the Holy Spirit. (1 Cor. 3:16; 6:19; 2 Cor. 6:16.) God lives in you. Christ dwells in you.

Does Jesus love Sam or Sally? With a perfect love! That's the only love you will ever get for Sam or Sally — and it is enough.

The Christian prayer is, "Father, I thank You that Christ loves Sam/Sally perfectly, and that Your Holy Spirit lives in me, and that therefore I have Christ's love for Sam/Sally in me. Forgive me for not understanding this enough and for not manifesting it enough. Thank You that it is really here. Now help me to eliminate whatever is hindering Christ's love from pouring through me to Sam/Sally."

Not "Positive Thinking"

This is not "positive thinking." It is the opposite of the kind of mental attitude that implies, "I don't quite have it yet [whatever "*it*" is], but if I reach out far enough, and high enough, and keep at it long enough, one of these days I may get it, or get more of it."

How depressing and negative such "positive thinking" is! How much more truly positive is the Christian message — that we really *do have* "it" — that we really do have Christ and all of His attributes in us: "Christ Jesus, whom God made our wisdom, our righteousness and sanctification and redemption" (1 Cor. 1:30 RSV).

If you are not a Christian, this principle does not apply. For you it *would* make sense to ask God to give you joy or peace or love. The right prayer, however, is to ask God to give you Jesus Christ. You get all of these blessings when you get Christ. The Scriptures are full of what we receive in Him.

What We Have in Christ

Actions — Ephesians 2:8,10; Philippians 2:13

Faith — Galatians 2:20; 5:22 KJV

Honor — 1 Chronicles 29:12; John 12:26

Life — Job 34:14,15; John 6:47

Patience — Galatians 5:22

Power — 2 Corinthians 13:4; Ephesians 3:20

Prayer — Romans 8:26

Strength — 1 Chronicles 29:12; Philippians 4:13

Thoughts — 1 Corinthians 2:16

Wealth — Deuteronomy 8:18; 1 Chronicles 29:12; Philippians 4:19

Will — Philippians 2:13

Wisdom — 1 Corinthians 1:30

Words — 2 Corinthians 13:3

Application to Everyday Life

A man with a withered hand was standing before Jesus wanting to be healed. (Matt. 12:9,10.) Jesus could have told him to go pray a certain prayer. The man could have done that, because his mouth muscles were working all right. Jesus could have told him to go to the temple. The man could have done that; his leg muscles were functioning. Jesus could have told him to go read a portion of Scripture. The man could have done that; his eye muscles were okay. Jesus told him to do *the one thing* that he could *not* do: "Stretch out your hand!"

Put yourself in the place of the man with the withered hand. What would you have thought? Perhaps you would have been tempted to say, "Well, Lord, I don't think You quite understand — that's the reason I'm here. You'll just have to do a miracle in my case." The Lord was going to do a miracle, but the man was to be involved.

Perhaps the man looked up into the face of Jesus and thought, "When this man commands me to stretch out my hand, I get the strange feeling that maybe I can. By the power of God or whatever it is I see in this man, I determine that I will obey and stretch out my hand. And here and now I do stretch out my hand!" He did — and the healing took place. (Matt. 12:10-13.)

When you read one of these Amazing Commands that you are to take control of your inner attitudes, inner feelings and emotions, inner experiences, such as the command to rejoice, are you tempted to think, "Well, Lord, I don't think You quite understand. I'm just not a very joyful person. You'll have to do a miracle in my case." He is ready and willing to do the miracle, but you are to be involved.

Are you willing to look into the face of Jesus and think, "When He commands me to rejoice, I get the strange feeling that maybe I can. I determine that I will obey and rejoice. And here and now I do rejoice!" When you do, you find the miracle of Christian living taking place.

The results may not always come that quickly, but you can quickly commit yourself to the process of learning that particular emotion. Sometimes "miracles" increase gradually as a development over a period of time, if we are willing to choose them and cultivate them.

The more we go through these kinds of experiences with the Lord in all of these areas, the more they become habitual. This principle of obedience to the Amazing Commands is illustrated in other encounters with Jesus, such as the man with crippled feet (Acts 3:1-8,16) who was commanded to stand up, the paralytic who was commanded to pick up his bed and walk (Mark 2:1-12) and even Lazarus who was commanded to rise from the dead. (John 11:41-44.)

Commitment and Process

Obedience to the Amazing Commands of God about emotions consists of both *commitment* and *process.* We commit ourselves *once and for all* to the principle, to the concept, to the belief that we can obey, by God's grace in us. The *process* of implementing the commitment in our daily lives involves a lifetime of growing, developing, increasing.

We probably don't go through the growing process until we commit ourselves to the principle. If we commit ourselves to the principle, we do make growth and progress in living it out.

If we don't commit ourselves to the principle of Christ's attributes in us, the slips in our daily lives are seen as inadequacies in us and pull us farther down. If we make the commitment to the principle, then the slips can pull us up by reminding us once again of what we are committed to and what we do have the potential for in our oneness with Christ.

How do we get slips to pull us up rather than down? By commitment. Without the commitment, we tend to respond to the slips with, "There I go again — I'm so stupid [inadequate, clumsy, worthless, etc.]." The slip produces the 8,563rd mental rehearsal of the destructive pattern with its reinforcement as the result of such repetition.

On the other hand, with the commitment having been made once and for all, then we tend to respond to the slip with, "That's not what I'm committed to. What I'm committed to is _____" — followed by the 9,842nd mental rehearsal of the commitment with its reinforcement.

The Inner Being, the Heart, the Attitudes

We are not minimizing the fact that the Scriptures do also encourage behavior, action, performance, deeds, etc. A greater emphasis, however, is upon *inner* emotions, feelings, attitudes, spirit and "gut level" experiences. (See 1 Samuel 16:7 and Appendix C.)

On the surface, the Pharisees were "good" people; they were moral, disciplined, well behaved, consistent, sincere and dedicated. Paul, the apostle, had been a Pharisee and had learned a great deal from them about piety, zeal and obedience to God. The problem was that their emphasis was only on the *outer* behavior, not upon the *inner* being.

One example from our counseling is the woman who attended about ten sessions, trying to decide whether or not to get a divorce. She had been married for many years. She came from a strong Christian background and professed to be a believer. Finally she came in one day and announced that she had made her decision. She had thoroughly studied the Bible and was determined to "obey the Word of God, and not get a divorce."

However, she was hostile, angry, bitter and vengeful. *But* she was "going to obey God's commands in His Word" and not file for divorce. She was failing to see that the Bible

70

not only commands us to behave in certain ways, such as not to divorce our mate, but that it also commands us, even if we don't get a divorce, to have inner peace, joy, harmony, composure, emotional stability, love, contentment, etc. It was almost as if, since she had chosen to obey the command of God in terms of overt behavior, she then had a right to disobey the commands of God concerning inner attitude.

The commands of God are *not multiple choice.* We may not pick and choose which ones to obey. If, as Christians, we profess to believe God and to follow Christ, we are obligated to take all the commands of God as a package. The Bible puts more emphasis on inner emotion than on physical behavior. With that understanding, would you be willing, on the following page, to sign your name to these commitments?

Date_____

1. I HEREBY COMMIT MYSELF TO THE PRINCIPLE OF OBEYING GOD'S COMMAND TO DEVELOP HEALTHY EMOTIONS.

2. WHEN I SLIP AND DISOBEY AND DO EXPERIENCE UNHEALTHY EMOTIONS, I HEREBY COMMIT MYSELF NOT TO BLAME THEM ON ANYBODY OR ANYTHING BUT TO ACCEPT MY OWN ACCOUNTABILITY FOR THEM.

3. WHEN I SLIP AND DO BLAME MY UNHEALTHY EMOTIONS ON ANYBODY OR ANYTHING, I HEREBY COMMIT MYSELF TO QUIT MAKING EXCUSES WHEN THE HOLY SPIRIT BRINGS IT TO MY REMEMBRANCE, AND TO REAFFIRM MY COMMITMENT TO ACCOUNTABLENESS.

SIGNED_____

If you have signed these commitments, then we are ready to move on to functional applications of them by understanding the two alternatives.

Chapter 5
THE TWO THEORIES —
THE REAL DIFFERENCES

The Bible starts with the idea that human beings are made in the image and likeness of God. (Gen. 1,2.) It does not make such a statement about the animals, only about human beings. According to this view, people are essentially different from the animals. For Christians, this biblical perspective is part of the Minority Point of View. The Majority take the opposite stance.

The Issues Involved in Making the Choice

The Minority Point of View, as discussed in the first three chapters, is that human beings are accountable for their responses. We are to face and accept the fact of our own primary and ultimate Accountableness for our own emotional feelings, attitudes and responses, whether or not we had a bad childhood, regardless of our heredity or environment and no matter how people and things were in the past or are in the present.

If we are accountable for our responses, the obvious implication is that we are to engage in ongoing, personal self-discipline in order to change any responses that are not right. We are to learn to make these changes even though people and things from the past and present may make it harder for us to respond in certain ways, and easier to respond in certain other ways. This responsibility may not be fair, but fairness is not the issue.

73

This Minority Theory is in contrast with the Majority Theory, which says that people and things from past and present *do cause* or *prevent* our emotional responses. The Majority assume that we are *controlled* by those past and outside forces. In that case we would not have the same Responsibleness for change. No wonder this theory is the Majority view! It allows us to let ourselves off the hook.

We need more descriptive names for the two conflicting perspectives than just Minority and Majority. Our preference is Accountableness or Responsibleness Theory as contrasted with Irresponsibleness Theory. Let's see why.

For Christians, the concept of being made in the image and likeness of God does become part of the Responsibleness Point of View. It is God who made us and gave us this genuine capacity for choosing and learning (or unlearning) our emotional responses, something which the animals, not being made in the image of God, do not have.

The Irresponsibleness Point of View does not accept this concept of human beings. The beliefs held by some scholars, such as Coon[1], by omission of any third factor beyond heredity and environment, and by omission of the influence of any spiritual factors, seem to undermine historic Bible beliefs such as those which hold that: 1) human beings are essentially different from the animals, not merely more complicated, 2) they are made in the image of God in a unique sense, 3) they do have responsibility for their own emotions, 4) they are shaped by more than the two factors of heredity and environment, 5) there is a third factor of genuine choice and 6) what appears to be choice is more than a chemical reaction produced by heredity and/or environment.

Which of these two alternatives is correct? Can either the Irresponsibleness Theory or the Responsibleness Theory be proven with scientific methods, with the slide rule, the test tube, etc.? No, each concept is simply a philosophical hypothesis. We simply choose and begin with one or the other. Then, on the basis of results, we decide whether to continue with the one we have chosen. Let's look at the implications of both, starting with the Responsibleness or Accountableness Theory.

Fifty-One Percent Means Control

Consider this analogy: if a person owns 51% or more of the common stock of a corporation he controls that company. He doesn't need to own 100%. The people who own the rest of the stock, even as much as 49%, may want to help. The 51% owner can afford to let the others have some say. He might even put some of them on the payroll or on the board of directors. He can accept their input in a relaxed, secure, confident way. He knows that, ultimately, he can outvote any of them, or all of them put together, as long as his actions are legal.

The process involved in a "hostile take-over" of a corporation is simple. If a person can buy up 51% of the voting stock, he can assume controlling interest in the firm. If less than half of the company's stock is all that is ever placed on the free market, then it will be impossible for him or anyone else to seize control. The way for any company to avoid being taken over is never to sell off more than 49% of its stock.

This analogy, applied to the concept of our being made in the image of God and thus different from the animals, suggests that we own 51% of our inner emotions, feelings, attitudes, responses and spirit. We have final responsibility for these things inside of us. We have the final control, authority and choice as to continuing with our usual inner emotional experiences or choosing and learning to change them.

The only exception to this ultimate Accountableness occurs when enough of the brain has been damaged or destroyed so that an individual no longer has genuine control over his own inner responses or the ability to learn how to change them. Disease, injury, surgery, birth defects, drugs, etc., can destroy enough brain cells that an individual becomes, in this sense, subhuman.

Other than these physical brain cell factors, a person cannot give away or "sell" his 51% ownership. It may appear so when one lets another make decisions for him — but that action is a choice and can be revoked by choice.

On the other hand, overt, *physical behavior can* be limited by genetics and conditioning, that is, by heredity and environment. But a person's ability to choose and learn his own *inner* emotional responses is still intact. Otherwise, how could God hold us accountable for them in a manner beyond what He does for the physical actions, as we saw in Chapter 4?

As we pointed out in that chapter, this genuine choice may not be, and usually is not, instantaneous. It may not be exercised easily, quickly or totally. But the buildup of choices can be unbuilt, or rebuilt, and changed through the choosing and cultivating process.

If you own 51% of the stock of the corporation of your own emotional responses, no one or no thing can ultimately execute a "take-over." You do outvote them all, at least ultimately. This is the Accountableness Theory.

The Third Factor

In this Minority Point of View, there is a third factor beyond heredity and environment. The great majority of writings in newspapers, journals, books and other media and forums are based on an assumption of only the two factors of heredity and environment. This is what we term the Majority Theory or the Irresponsibleness Theory.

One author writes a book "proving" that our emotional responses are *not* caused by our environment. For those who accept that argument it seems very obvious that what controls our emotional responses is, therefore, *of course*, heredity, genetics, nature, inborn factors.

Then another author comes along and writes a book "proving" that our emotional responses are *not* caused by heredity. For those who accept this argument, therefore, *of course*, it seems perfectly clear that the determining factor must be environment, conditioning, nurture.

For three generations our society has been subjected to this Irresponsibleness concept and as a result has been talked into rejecting the third factor of choice and cultivation.[2] That Majority, who believe that emotional responses are caused or prevented exclusively by these background factors, must of course reject the 51% Principle — the genuine choice, the Accountableness, the third factor, the self-discipline of learning, being made in the image of God — what we call Responsibleness.

No, "reject" may be too strong a word. Usually these people simply ignore the third factor of choice and cultivation. Perhaps even "ignore" is too strong a word. Our generation, approximately the third since the Majority view has been the dominant one, often does not even possess in their "computers" — in their brains, in their awareness — the concept of choice and cultivation. For them, it simply does not exist.

They argue back and forth whether the dominant factor in determining emotional responses is heredity, or whether it is environment, or whether it is in some way both. For them, choice and cultivation simply *do not exist*. If "choice" is a word in their vocabularies, it is thought of simply as denoting a chemical reaction related to heredity and/or environment — and therefore does not constitute a genuine choice.

If we seem to be overstating this ignoring of the third factor by the Majority, we have a suggestion for you. Dear Abby and Ann Landers have their fingers on the emotional pulse of the majority of Americans. Read either of their columns regularly and see how the only two factors usually considered are heredity and/or environment.

In the letters asking for advice you will see that if it is not environment controlling our responses, then it is of course heredity — if it is not heredity controlling our responses, then it is of course environment. According to the Irresponsibleness Theory, what else could it possibly be? It is considered to be, *of course,* one or the other or both. Many college textbooks amplify this dualism even more thoroughly than the daily newspapers.

A personal note: I was forty years old and had been a Christian for twenty-five years before I even heard (as I remember) about the true dominance of the third factor of choice and cultivation. All I had ever heard was heredity and/or environment. I had earned a bachelor's degree, a master's degree and a Ph.D. degree from three of the finest universities in the country. I had attended theological seminary and was ordained. I was a diligent Bible student and read widely — yet I had never encountered this simple alternative concept.

Implications for America

When the Minority Theory of choice and cultivation is presented to the Majority, many of them reject it vigorously. They insist on considering nothing but heredity and environment. Later in this book we will discuss reasons why some people apparently reject the Accountableness Theory — and not just because they are unaware of it. Their commitment to nothing but heredity and environment and the vehemence with which they reject choice and cultivation suggest that they are using a "red herring" — a diversionary tactic to avoid something that is personally unpleasant to them.

I heard a psychology professor give a series of lectures in which one of the main themes was, "We must not let the Existentialists and the Christians drag back a third force in personality theory. We must stick to our guns, that people are a product of two and only two forces, heredity and environment. The moment we allow any third factor, we open the floodgates to the return of the feelings of guilt that we have so successfully eliminated in these last few decades."

I pursued the subject further with the professor. I asked why he made no place in his system for a third factor. He asked what I meant. I answered: "Individuality, initiative, independence, imagination, accountability, creativity, choice, learning, will, freedom, responsibility . . ." He interrupted and said bluntly, "Scientifically, those are meaningless concepts."

Such response depends on one's definition of science. If one means, by science, only that which can be measured with laboratory techniques, there may be some merit in his statements. These factors cannot be measured as obviously as heredity and environment. But that is a limited view of science. If there is any one factor that has made America great, it is that we have taken seriously the concepts of individual choice and responsibility. We need to think fast and work hard to prevent the Majority from taking away from us this precious heritage of Accountableness.[3]

Some of us who accept the Minority Theory do so because we sincerely believe that it is what the Bible teaches. Another reason some of do so is that we do not like the feeling of being victims. If one is a product of nothing but his heredity and his environment, then he really does have no choice — and he is a helpless victim of his circumstances.

Admittedly, embracing the Responsibleness Theory has some discomfort too. For us as Christians it means that we are "doomed" to lives of emotional self-discipline, to a neverending task of increasingly bringing our emotions as well as our behavior in line with Scripture and what is pleasing to God. Some of us then see that self-discipline, as "painful" as it may be, is not as painful as being a victim.

Rejecting the Majority Theory

A pair of identical twins had an alcoholic father. One twin became, like his father, an alcoholic. The other twin became an abstainer. The psychologist working with both twins asked privately of the alcoholic twin, "Do you know why you became an alcoholic?"

The alcoholic twin answered, "With a father like I had, what else would you expect?"

The psychologist separately and privately asked the other twin, "Do you know why you became an abstainer?"

The abstainer twin answered, "With a father like I had, what else would you expect?"

Both twins had the same heredity and approximately the same environmental conditioning.

One chose to go along with his heredity and/or environment. The other chose to go the opposite way from his heredity and/or environment.

It may have been harder for the abstainer twin to depart from his heredity and/or environment than it was for the alcoholic twin to go along with his heredity and/or environment.

This argument is usually the final one that the Majority make in response to the Responsibleness Theory — "It isn't fair!" We agree that it is not fair for it to be harder for one than for another other. However, in this book we are not attempting to address the issue of fairness. We are addressing issues of effectiveness, efficiency, productivity, performance, enjoyment, spontaneity, motivation, alertness, energy, emotional control, etc., regardless of what is fair or unfair.

Ella Wheeler Wilcox put it poetically:

One ship sails east and one ship sails west
　　With the self-same winds that blow.
'Tis the set of the sails and not the gales
　　That tells where the ship will go.
Like the winds of the sea are the winds of fate
　　As we voyage along through life.
'Tis the set of a soul that decides its goal
　　And not the calm or the strife.[4]

In each of our lives there are people, places, things, and situations that are placing "winds of pressure" upon us. The ultimate goal — after we have changed those things (Option I) or avoided those things which we can and should change or avoid (Option II) — is to face and accept the fact of our Accountableness for our responses, whatever the pressures. For the Christian, the set of the sail and the rudder, the "set of the soul," depends on the guidance of the Word of God and the indwelling presence and power of the Spirit of God.

The Apostle Paul put it in a more specifically Christian sense:

Not that I speak in regard to need, for I have learned in whatever state I am, to be content:

I know how to be abased, and I know how to abound. Everywhere and in all things I have learned both to be full and to be hungry, both to abound and to suffer need.

I can do all things through Christ who strengthens me.

Philippians 4:11-13

In verse 12, Paul uses a special Greek word, *mueo*, for "learned." It is the only time this word is used in the entire New Testament. It is taken from the pagan philosophers but sanctified with Christian meaning by verse 13. Barclay calls it "One of the great words of pagan ethnics" but "Christianity succeeds because it was rooted in the divine."[5]

Translators, lexicographers and commentators feel obligated to include more than just the word "learned." Most add at least the phrase "the secret" or "I have learned the secret" following the R.V. Most add even more details. For example:

"I've been very thoroughly initiated into the human lot." "I have been initiated into all the mysteries of life." He had gone through "the rites of admission to a secret society."[6]

"There is a secret way to live."[7]

"In any and in all circumstances I have learned the secret."[8]

"Instruct in the sacred mysteries . . . a secret which would remain such but for revelation."[9]

"I have learned the secret . . . I am initiated. I possess the mystery."[10]

"I have been initiated, I possess the secret."[11]

"I have mastered the secret of all conditions."[12]

"I have learned . . . the secret of facing every situation."[13]

"He has learned in the school of life."[14]

"I have learned the secret . . . the secret of risky Christianity . . . anywhere, at any time."[15]

"To initiate into the mysteries. . . . to teach fully . . . to give one an intimate acquaintance with a thing. . . . in everything and in all things I have learned the secret."[16]

"I am fully initiated into all the secrets."[17]

"I have been initiated into the secret for all sorts and conditions of life."[18]

Perhaps the simplest way of putting a lot of these interpretations together might be: "I have learned the true secret of life." That secret then is:

By God's empowering grace, we can handle our inner responses regardless of tangible circumstances or events.

The Christian Difference

Wilcox's poem could leave people somewhat threatened, even Christians. And it should! However, the same concept becomes uplifting and inspiring and encouraging when taken in conjunction with Paul's last phrase that by Christ's strength in us we can handle the ups and the downs of life — being abased and abounding, experiencing fullness and enduring hunger, enjoying abundance and suffering need, etc.

Some people, reading Paul's message superficially, see it as just one more of those many passages in Scripture of learning to bear hardships. This passage is different. Paul is talking about the art of accepting the good as well as the bad.

So what is the art of accepting the good? Cannot anyone do that? Paul is saying, first of all, of course, that we are not to blame others for our miseries. However, he is also saying, and it is just as important, that we are not to hold others accountable for our inner peace, contentment, joy, emotional strength and stability, poise and composure, happiness.

It is important to recognize that we may not handle well this Accountableness quickly, easily or totally, but that by God's grace we can do it increasingly. As evidence, let's look at how others have done it.

Chapter 6
FUNCTIONAL APPLICATIONS
OF
THE ACCOUNTABLENESS
THEORY

A men's service club asked me to be the speaker at their weekly luncheon. The program chairman suggested that the members would be interested in hearing some of our views on Responsibleness Theory — what I call the 51% Principle, or Option III, the facing and accepting of one's own Accountableness for his own responses, whatever the circumstances.

This theme can be understood by anyone who is willing, regardless of his religion. As a Christian, I am convinced that it takes the grace of God to handle this Accountableness well. However, with a secular group, I start only with the accountability principle as such.

Accountableness Not New

The talk was received well. Several of the members came up afterward to make comments or ask questions. One man, referring to the Responsibleness Theory, wondered how I had been able to "come up with such a fresh, new idea about human behavior." I pointed out that some of the greatest thinkers of all ages and all walks of life had stated the same theme. He was surprised. I offered to send him some quotations from my files. Some of these quotations are as follows:

Quotations on Individual Choice and Accountability

The fountain of content must spring up in the mind, and he who has so little knowledge of human nature as to seek happiness by changing anything but his own disposition will waste his life in fruitless efforts and multiply the griefs which he purposes to remove.

— Samuel Johnson

People can find happiness only for themselves. . . . Happiness occurs most often when we are willing to take responsibility for our behavior. Irresponsible people, always seeking to gain happiness without assuming responsibility, find only brief periods of joy, but not the deep-seated satisfaction which accompanies responsible behavior.[1]

— William Glasser, M.D.

An optimist is a person who sees a green light everywhere. The pessimist sees only the red light. But the truly wise person is color-blind.

— Dr. Albert Schweitzer

The happiness of your life depends on the quality of your thoughts; therefore guard accordingly, and take care that you entertain no notions unsuitable to virtue and reasonable nature.

— Marcus Antonius
Roman Emperor (A.D. 121-180)

. . . man is about as happy as he makes up his mind to be.

— Abraham Lincoln

> Nothing can work me damage . . . except myself.
> . . . The harm I sustain I carry about with me . . . and
> am never a real sufferer but by my own fault.

> — Saint Bernard

> God give me the courage to change what can be
> changed, the serenity to accept what cannot be
> changed, and the wisdom to know the difference.[2]

(For the remainder of the quotes, see Appendix D.)

I did also include the Philippians 4 quotation from the Apostle Paul that was discussed in the preceding chapter of this book. I included this quote because, if the man were a Christian, it would be meaningful for him to be reminded that Christ in him was the enabling power to handle increasingly well his own Accountableness. (See Appendixes A and B.) And if he were not a Christian, then, after thinking through the "accountability theme," he might be wondering whether he had the capability to apply it. If so, he might be ready to see that taking Christ into his life is what would give him that capability.

We believe in presenting all of the commands of Scripture, including the Amazing Commands, those which deal with inner emotions. We present these even to the non-Christian. In the book of Galatians, Paul points out that the commands of God can be a convicting experience for the nonbeliever, and thereby become a "schoolmaster" to bring him to Christ. (Gal. 3:19-25 KJV.)

It is important to see both of these two distinct themes — *accountability* and *capability*.

Even though the Accountableness Theory is a Minority Theory, many people believe it who are not necessarily Christians. As mentioned earlier, Jean-Paul Sartre, the leading Existentialist, believed in the accountability concept. The final conclusion of this gifted thinker was that: yes, we are accountable for our inner responses, but we can't handle that accountability! What he didn't see was that it does take Christ.

Some modern approaches other than the biblical approach do take seriously the fact of accountability for one's own emotional responses — Glasser[3] with Reality Therapy, Berne[4] and Harris[5] with Transactional Analysis, Frankl[6] with Logotherapy, Ellis[7] with Rational-Emotive Therapy, and others from Cognitive Therapies,[8] Existentialism,[9] Humanism,[10] Holism,[11] etc. One problem with most of them is that while they take accountability seriously, their methods of handling that accountability fall short without a serious acceptance of God's empowering grace and enablement. Some who do emphasize this acceptance, for example, are D. Martyn-Lloyd Jones,[12] Pierre Teilhard de Chardin,[13] Paul Tournier[14] and J. Wesley Bready.[15]

The Ignoring of the Minority Theory

Perhaps the intuitive sense that we are not capable of handling this inner accountability is one of the reasons why it is so ignored — ignored to the point of oblivion, ignored to the point where, for all practical purposes, it doesn't exist.

A working committee of thirty people were planning and preparing six half-hour video tapes to be used for pre-retirement planning. Lawyers, doctors, recreational professionals, accountants, housing specialists, transportation experts, and representatives from various walks of life were included. One woman and I were included as "representatives of the Mental Health Field."

During the first three meetings, she and I tried to assert our plea for one of the tapes to include methods of working on *attitudes* in retirement and in preparation for retirement. We were mostly ignored.

Toward the end of the third session, the agenda for the six tapes was becoming finalized. I made one last, vigorous plea that one of the tapes should be on "mental health," using their term. The room got quiet. One of the sociologists, apparently somewhat offended, said, "Dr. Lantz, everything we have been talking about contributes to mental health."

I tried to remain calm but firm: "No, everyone here knows that the definition of mental health is: the inner emotional strength and stability which one cultivates inside himself, regardless of the contributions from outside."

Since the room was still quiet, I decided to go all the way: "In fact, mental health is that inner composure and emotional well-being, even when the contributions from outside are all bad!"

Up to that point, this concept had not existed in their conscious minds. Yet once I stated it, at the right moment, not a person denied it. The result was that one of the six tapes was on "mental health," and our agency was the major organizer and contributor.

Excellent training programs resulted, including planning for retirement, handling of changes in financial status, the trauma of changes in the family situation, learning to cope with physical difficulties, the legal issues, the social issues, etc. Included in my agency's tape were ways of handling inner emotions, attitudes, feelings and moods, even when these other tangible realities were not what they should be.

Denying the Minority Theory

We have thus seen that some people ignore this Minority Theory of accountability. For them, Responsibleness doesn't exist; it is not among the thirty trillion pieces of data in their computer which we call the brain.

However, some can't seem to ignore it, but they use evasive tactics to avoid dealing with it. The day after Sirhan

Sirhan assassinated Robert Kennedy, one commentator on national television said, "Every single one of us in America is equally guilty with this man because we have created a society which produces this kind of personality."

Our society does have ills. I will take my share of the blame for those ills and my share of the responsibility for doing something about them. However, many people who grew up in the same society that Sirhan did, bad as it was, don't go around killing people. No matter how bad the influence upon us may be, each one of us still has the primary and ultimate responsibility for how he responds, even though it is harder for some than for others — and even though it's not fair for it to be harder.

Examples of the Minority Theory

Robert Stroud, "the Birdman of Alcatraz," was violent and hostile when the guards put him in prison.[16] Eventually it became clear to him that, yes, they could control his environment, and yes, they could control his body, but he was not an animal. They did not have control over his inner spirit, his inner responses.

When this became evident to him, he became one of the world's leading ornithologists (bird experts) while still in prison. But more important to the issues with which we are dealing, he became a man of inner harmony, inner composure and inner emotional strength and stability.

Irony occurred in the fact that some of his captors thought they could get control of the Birdman's attitudes and tried to do so. Ultimately, they were the ones who became frustrated, rather than the Birdman. Stroud found a freedom of sorts — a freedom of the spirit. His captors were the ones who were really in "prison" — feeling tension, stress and pressure because they could not get the emotional control they wanted of another person.

An example with the Christian perspective is Corrie ten Boom.[17] Confined to a Nazi prison camp during World War II, she became bitter and hostile. Her sister, Betsy, was with her but understood the principle of individual choice and accountability. As bad as the situation was, Betsy learned, by God's grace and enablement, to keep her sanity, her composure, her emotional equilibrium.

Corrie and some of the other Christian friends could not understand Betsy. They were confused; they knew that Betsy did not *approve* of what the Nazis were doing. Yet, to them, if a person disapproved, as any Christian should, he would be filled with rage and vengefulness.

Motivation for Changing Emotions

Betsy's perspective was that bitterness, rage, vengefulness, etc., were not enjoyable (if anything, interfered with her joy), were not adding to her effectiveness (if anything, were hindering it), were not promoting her physical health (if anything, were lessening it), were not pleasing to God (if anything, were displeasing Him) — so why choose to continue the bitterness and other negative inner responses?

Finally, Corrie understood, and she learned to keep her composure in spite of what the Nazis were doing. Keeping her poise and inner harmony did not cause her to become more of a doormat — just the opposite. She became more effective in dealing with her oppressors. She also became more effective with her associates, and ultimately with other people all over the world. After she was released from the prison camp, she traveled around the world for more than three decades, preaching the Gospel.

She understood her Accountableness for her own inner attitudes, and she utilized the special grace of God's enablement to handle the Responsibleness well. The captors of Corrie and the Birdman believed that they could control the attitudes of their captives. The captors did not believe the 49%-51% Principle. They did not understand that they did not have the final ability to manipulate their captives' attitudes. They, themselves became the frustrated ones and were the real "captives."

Teaching Accountableness to Children

The space shuttle explosion in 1987 killed all the astronauts on board, including a schoolteacher. Because a teacher was going into space for the first time, children across the nation were more involved. They were at their schools, with their teachers, watching the television broadcast of the take-off, when the fatal mishap occurred.

For the next day or so, teachers, parents, psychologists and various social, educational and mental-health professionals were wringing their hands with dismay. They lamented that this traumatic event would scar these poor children for life.

To let children know that you expect a traumatic event to scar them for life is the worst message you can communicate to them. This implication is handing to the children on a silver platter the most weaseling, buck-passing "cop out" possible. For the rest of their lives, any "goof ups" they make can be blamed on this traumatic event that was a part of their childhood.

After a day or two, many of these adults chose to quit the panic. They confidently promised, "We will go to these children and give them counseling, tutoring, relationship and other forms of influence. We will prevent this event from scarring these children for life."

On the surface, this second reaction may seem better. Actually, it is worse. It is more subtle. In response to any problem these children have, for the rest of their lives, they can say, "Those people did not do enough for us to prevent us from being scarred for life."

So what is the answer? We start with trying to communicate to the children, "How you respond to this event is ultimately and primarily your own responsibility." If the children choose to face and accept the fact of their own ultimate and primary Accountableness for their responses, then what we say will not do harm, and may do some good. If the children choose not to face and accept the fact of their own ultimate and primary Accountableness for their own responses, then what we say will not do any good, and may do harm.

But can a school-aged child understand this principle? Yes, even a preschooler can understand it. The parent of a three- or four-year-old can state the summary of this entire book in one sentence:

"Sally, how long do you choose to stay angry?"

"Sammy, how long do you choose to stay pouting?"

"Johnny, how long do you choose to stay sad?"

"Janie, how long do you choose to stay afraid?"

One parent of a three-and-one-half-year-old had used this kind of a sentence with the child several times but was not sure whether the question was getting through. Finally the parent asked, "Sally, how long do you choose to stay angry?"

Sally paused a moment, then answered, "Oh, maybe ten minutes, and then I'll decide to feel okay again."

The message of Accountableness may have been starting to get through.

Parenting and Handling Children

If the child does have Accountableness, if he owns 51% of the common stock of his company, if Option III is always there as a last resort, if good emotions are an act of obedience to God and if he is responsible to make conscious and healthy choices about his emotions as well as his actions, then it becomes obvious to the parent that the parent never owns more than 49%.

The art of parenting is not to try to manipulate or control to get more than 49%. It is to make the most artistic, creative and godly use of the 49%. Later in this book, we will have a whole chapter on the 49% Principle.

Meanwhile, however, let's consider one good example. A woman, who was in charge of the children in her church on Sunday mornings and other times, came to me with tears in her eyes. She said that I would just have to help her control those kids, to make them behave, to force them to "shape up."

I tried to explain some of the ways to influence children, but none of them satisfied her because they did not give her the final control, never helped her to own more than 49%. After each suggestion I gave and she rejected, she tried to answer her own question:

"Do you think if I spend more time with them, that will change them?

"If I love them enough, surely that will force them to behave, won't it?

"If I just teach them well, won't that make them shape up?"

I just repeated Accountableness. She thought I was teasing her. She pleaded, "Please tell me; I really must know!"

Finally I reminded her that based on her own concepts, Judas' betrayal was Jesus' fault. If Jesus had spent more time with Judas, if He had loved Judas more, if He had taught Judas well enough, then Judas would not have betrayed Him. Even Jesus won only eleven out of twelve. I told her that she was trying to outdo Jesus.

She was shocked and said that she would need some time to think about it. She came back a few weeks later and exclaimed that this concept was to her a completely new way of dealing with children. Remember, we have admitted, even insisted, that it is the Minority Point of View.

We are certainly accountable for what we teach children and how we treat them, but they have the ultimate and final accountability for whether they choose to learn or accept.

The Majority usually ask, "But what *causes* the child to accept or reject?" If something is *causing* his response, this is a denial of genuine choice, of free will, of being made in the image of God, of accountability, of responsibility, of the reality of God's commands and enablement, of the entire Word of God.

I frequently counsel managers, policemen, teachers and others who are in positions of leadership or authority. They often are positive that there is some way to *make* their students, employees, citizens or others under their leadership do something, that there must be some way to control them, to force them to change, to make them respond in a certain way.

Unlocking the Majority

When one of these persons is locked into that Majority Theory, it is sometimes impossible to help him to see any other alternative. In a class, or just in general contacts, especially when the person is angry, all we can do is try to help him work out his problem in some slight practical way in his own thinking and actions, as follows.

In counseling, when a person has come seeking help, but has genuine difficulty giving up the Majority Theory that people and things from the past and the present are controlling his responses, that is, preventing some and causing others, there is a way to get around his problem.

Both positions are only theories. The Minority Theory of Responsibleness is one theory. The Majority Theory of Irresponsibleness is another. Neither of them can be proved.

We point out to the counselee that, based upon his Majority Theory, we cannot be of help to him in our counseling. We cannot change for him those things that are supposedly controlling his responses. The only way we can be of help to him is if he is *willing* to let us *operate* upon the Accountability Theory for the time being.

It is only when a person at least allows us to *operate* on the concept of accountability that he does anything about changing his own responses. We can help him if he is willing to let us operate, even temporarily and tentatively, with him viewing his responses in light of his own Accountableness, and with God's empowering, making some changes.

In this entire book, we are not really trying to *convince* you, the reader, that the Minority Theory is true and the Majority Theory is false. We cannot prove that to you. All we are saying is that if you wish to make changes in your own responses, you probably will not do so until you at least try operating on the Accountableness Theory. One way to compare the two theories is by looking at what we do expect to get from people and things, and what we don't expect to get from them.

Chapter 7
WHAT WE GET FROM OUTSIDE

Let us look at what we do not get from the outside. Consider again, more in depth, Samuel Johnson's statement from the preceding chapter.

> The fountain of content must spring up in the mind, and he who has so little knowledge of human nature as to seek happiness by changing anything but his own disposition will waste his life in fruitless efforts and multiply the griefs which he purposes to remove.

"The fountain of content must spring up [not in the job, church, community, home, etc. but] in the mind [in each person's mind], and he who has so little knowledge of human nature as to seek happiness by changing anything [job, church, community, family, etc.] but his own disposition will waste his life in fruitless efforts . . . [If Johnson had stopped there, it would be jolting enough. Up to this point he is saying that as long as we rely on anybody or anything outside ourselves for our inner joy, we won't find it. It gets worse as he continues] . . . and multiply the griefs which he purposes to remove."

As long as we rely on anybody or anything outside ourselves for our inner peace and joy, we not only don't have a chance of finding it, we will only get more and more miserable as time goes by.

Johnson is not saying that we shouldn't try to change anything. He was a world-changer and a people-changer.

He is saying that we are not to see control of our inner emotions, responses and attitudes as dependent on whether or not we change people and things either present or past.

Nor is Johnson saying that we should expect to be happy continuously. The point is that, when we are unhappy or miserable, we do not place the blame on anybody or anything, but take responsibility for it ourselves.

Happiness Is Not a By-Product

Did our Founding Fathers offer us life, liberty and happiness? No, they knew better. They offered us simply the *pursuit* of happiness. Each individual is responsible for his own emotional condition.

A common view is that happiness is a by-product.[1] This idea is a direct application of the Majority Theory — that people and things from past and present determine our emotions. God commands us to make up our minds to be happy and then implement that decision through a process of discipline. Happiness is a choice, not a by-product. It is chosen and learned.

Anyone who teaches, "Don't ever seek happiness — just do those things that produce happiness," is teaching contrary to Scripture and God's commands.

Do Change Things

The Apostle Paul's point is similar to Johnson's. In the quotation from Philippians, Chapter 4 (previously discussed), Paul is not saying that we should not try to change anything or anybody. He is saying that we should not let our contentment depend on whether or not we can bring about change on the outside. We can still bring about change on the inside, by God's grace, regardless of external circumstances.

The Serenity Prayer of Alcoholics Anonymous and Al-Anon quoted in Chapter 6 begins by asking God to give us the courage to change things that can be changed, but concludes with the acknowledgment that our serenity does not depend on what can or cannot be changed externally.

What Can We Get?

Nor are any of these people we have quoted saying that we should not expect to get anything from anybody or anything outside ourselves. What do we have a right to expect? Let's start with the closest relationship, marriage.

Sam did not marry Sally just for Sally's benefit. But Sam knows that Sally did not marry him just for his benefit. Part of the reason an individual enters and remains in a marital relationship is for what he or she gets from it. What are some of the things a spouse might hope to get from a mate?

Consider the following list. Cross off anything you think not appropriate. Add anything you think is appropriate. Reword any of them the way you think they should be stated. In the final analysis, are these some of the kinds of things that you want to get from your marriage partner (or from others too in some cases)?

Benefits of a Relationship

Things you may get from and give to others.

Advice and counsel

Compensation, appreciation

Enjoyable companionship

Environmental freedom

Exciting recreation

Fair treatment

Fellowship, company

Food, shelter

Fulfilling sex
Fun-filled activities
Harmonious situation
Helpful provisions
Interesting conversation
Listening ear
Meaningful relationship
Payment, reward
Peaceful circumstances
Personal support
Physical care, comfort, security
Pleasure
Thrilling experiences

_____

(Other — write in)

Sometimes in the beginning of our marriage counseling, a spouse (let's call him Sam) will angrily mutter that he is not getting anything from that list. We can usually show him that this is not true, that he is getting at least some of these things. He then may argue that he is not getting enough of them. This attitude is obviously subjective; how can anyone say categorically what is enough of any of these tangibles?

He then usually considers himself to be conclusive when he announces that he can get more of these things somewhere else. This may be true, but we can sometimes help him see that by such thinking he is running a risk of sacrificing the investment he has made in his marriage relationship as well as violating his commitment to his spouse "for better or for worse."

More often than not, the real problem is *none* of those three objections: 1) that he is not getting any of these items, 2) that he is not getting enough of them, or 3) that he can get more of them elsewhere. The real issue usually lies in the two columns on the following page. (This is another perspective of the same two columns we looked at in Chapter 2.)

Emotional Analysis

Things you cannot get from or give to others (i.e., emotions you have learned or may choose to unlearn or learn).

_____fretful irritation
_____anxious disharmony
_____frustrated discouragement
_____miserable distress
_____inner conflict of pressure
_____insecure worry
_____fearful apprehension
_____angry wrath, "mad"
_____sad depression
_____hostile rage
_____nervous tension or strain
_____disgruntled upset
_____"bugged," "uptight"
_____ inner feelings of
   emptiness or bondage
_____ excessive emotions of
   guilt and inferiority
_____hopeless spirit
_____hurt feelings, self-pity
_____"torn up," discord
_____covetous envy

_____calm serenity
_____emotional stability and
   strength
_____tranquil spirit
_____peace of mind
_____inner experience of
   gladness and joy
_____good humor
_____emotion of
   contentment
_____inner harmony and
   composure
_____inner happiness
_____patience
_____relaxation
_____inner poise and
   steadiness
_____emotional feeling of
   fullness
_____emotional feeling of
   inner freedom
_____empathic warm regard
_____enthusiastic zeal
_____good desires, tastes,
   cravings

_____
(Other—write in)

_____
(Other—write in)

Most often Sam is saying that his mate is causing in him some of those emotions in the left column and not giving him any of those emotions in the right column. The most common complaint we hear in marriage counseling is, "My spouse is making me miserable," or "My spouse is not making me happy."

But note the subtitle of the preceding page. The items in the left column are not caused by one's mate, nor are the ones in the right column prevented by one's mate. Neither are the things on this double-column page controlled by job, church, friends, fellow employees or anyone else. These other people and things can contribute or hinder as much as 49%, but not 51%.

When our counselees get honest, their reasons for leaving a relationship or situation are usually found on the double-column page, not the single-column page, and are therefore inappropriate and invalid. It turns out that Sam's problem was not any of his original three objections: 1) that he was not getting any of the things on the single-column page, 2) that he was not getting enough of those things or 3) that he could get more of those things elsewhere.

Not: Happy About

Have you ever tried to cheer up a child when he is pouting, only to be asked by him: "How can I be happy unless there is something to be happy *about*?" The typical child, until he has learned this Accountableness lesson, assumes that the only way he can be happy is for somebody or something outside and beyond himself to make him happy. Remember the popular little books: *Happiness Is . . .* ?

Some people carry this false expectation on into adult life. Daniel, an intelligent and well-motivated business-man, came to us for counseling after his wife had committed against him the worst possible offenses, finally leaving him for another man. During a number of sessions, we went through our principles with him. He seemed to be understanding and applying them with dignity and poise.

Finally, one day, out of character, he pounded the arm of the chair and shouted, "Do you mean to tell me that I should be happy *about* what she's doing?" We were finally at the watershed issue. I had never suggested being happy *about* anything, but *in spite of* things.

I pointed out that his wife was doing bad things, and that he should not hide his eyes or kid himself into thinking she was not doing them. But I also assured him that he could keep his own inner peace and joy *anyhow, regardless of* the bad things she was doing, which he could not change, which he was not happy *about*, but could be happy *in spite of*.

Does it seem that it is hard to make yourself happy? It is not as hard as trying to get someone else to make you happy. Our emotional well-being does not come from people and things outside ourselves.

Think back to Ella Wheeler Wilcox's poem about the sailing ships (Chapter 5). When we look out on a lake and see a sailboat sailing in an easterly direction, we may think to ourselves, "The wind is blowing the ship east." This would not be exactly untrue.

However, we look again and see another ship sailing westward. We scratch our heads and wonder whether there are two different winds blowing that day. No, it is the same wind. But the wind does not determine ultimately which direction the ship goes. That is determined by the set of the sail and the rudder.

Every Christian has a rudder. It is the enablement of God, through His Word and the Holy Spirit, and other means of grace such as the fellowship of other believers. In spite of whichever way the wind is blowing us, we still can determine, by God's grace, which way we go.

Senior Citizens

I was serving on a community board to help with programming for some senior citizens' centers. It involved people from the fields of housing, recreation, transportation, nutrition, etc. My recommendation was in the area of working directly with seniors' attitudes.

I apparently pushed too hard one time and offended a member of the board. His pronouncement to me was: "If we get that bus there on time, a roof over their head that doesn't leak, a game that is lively, a hot meal once a day, then you won't have to worry about their attitudes. Their attitudes will take care of themselves."

His fallacy was so obvious, I didn't need to say another word to the committee. They knew that you can get the bus there on the dot, erect a solid roof over their heads, provide a fun game and serve up a hot meal, but some will still choose to be miserable. On the other hand, the bus can be a little late, the roof leak a bit, the game fall flat and the meal be cold, but some will still choose to be happy anyhow. *Both* alternatives disprove the Majority Theory.

I have spent a great deal of time working with senior citizens' projects. I have seen much of Samuel Johnson's point that those who fail to face the fact of their own Accountableness get more and more miserable as time goes by. I believe I can spend only a few minutes with a senior citizen and can tell which decision he has made. Whatever his decision, it seems to move him farther in that direction with the passage of time.

When the whole issue comes down to a decision, and when one honestly looks at the alternatives, the Majority Theory can readily be rejected. Let's see why.

Chapter 8
PROBLEMS WITH THE MAJORITY THEORY

The Majority Theory began in the Garden of Eden. God asked Adam: "Why did you eat the forbidden fruit?"

Adam answered: "The woman You created, Lord — *she* caused me to eat."

God said: "Eve, why did you eat the fruit?"

Eve replied: "The serpent You created, Lord — *he* caused me to eat." (Gen. 3:1-13.)

So the Majority Theory, the Irresponsibleness Theory — holding someone or something accountable for one's own responses — has been with us ever since the Fall of Man. This buck-passing approach to life is part of original sin. Original sin itself was disobeying and rebelling against God, partaking of the one tree from which God had commanded Adam and Eve not to eat. Immediately with the rebellion and disobedience came projection of blame, the "cop out" on Accountableness.

Adam and Eve, and their successors in this Irresponsibleness Theory, are not exactly fibbing. Eve really did tempt Adam, and the serpent really did tempt Eve. But *the point* of Genesis, Chapter 3, is that Adam and Eve both still owned 51% of the decision-making power. They were each supposed to have said: "No thanks!" And God held them accountable for their ownership of the 51% and for succumbing to the pressures placed upon them.

The Power of Heredity and Environment

Some of the Majority lean more heavily on heredity than on environment:

"That's just how I am . . . I was born this way . . . I inherited this tendency from my parents . . . You can't change human nature . . . You can't change how you feel . . . It's in my genes . . . I've always been this way."

Some of the Majority, on the other hand, lean more toward environment than toward heredity:

"That's the way I was brought up . . . I learned it from my father . . . I'm just a product of my mother's teaching . . . The devil made me do it . . . I had a bad childhood . . . I was never taught any better . . . That bugs me . . . It upsets me . . . They irritate me . . . He makes me mad . . . She scares me . . . Traffic makes me nervous . . . The boss drives me nuts . . . Sam ruins my day . . . Sally is giving me ulcers."

Let the Freudians, the Behaviorists, the Humanists and all others who espouse the Majority Theory not accuse the Minority of minimizing the power of heredity and/or environment. The serpent *did* make it harder for Eve to obey God, and Eve *did* make it harder for Adam.

The "Instinct" of Buck-Passing

Down through the ages, ever since Adam and Eve, people have continued, as part of the sinful nature of humanity, to do this buck-passing. It is intuitive. When the grade-schooler comes home with an "A" on his report card, he says, "Look at the grade I got!" When he gets a "C," he says, "Look at what the teacher gave me!" Who taught him this buck-passing? No one. It's instinctive; it's part of original sin.

When a businessman's stock investment goes up, he says, "Look at the stock I bought!" When the stock price goes down, he may say, "Look at what that broker sold me!"

When a worker's retirement turns out well, he says, "Look at what I built up!" When his retirement turns out badly, he may say, "Look at what the company did to me!"

I have worked with top executives as well as bums on skid row. The successful executive likes to think of himself as a "self-made" man. In a sense this is true — in that he has taken the primary responsibility for his own responses rather than holding someone or something else accountable. On the other hand, I don't ever recall a bum on skid row talking about himself as a "self-made" man. Rather the usual excuse is: "Look at what society has done to me."

So people have done this buck-passing down through the ages, but usually a little sheepishly, with a little embarrassment, because generally they have known intuitively that they really had the ultimate Accountableness.

A little embarrassment still persists among the Majority that we need to consider. It has not been totally eliminated even with the advent of the "scientific" approach, which they see as dealing only with heredity and environment, without considering any third factor of choice or accountability.

Embarrassment Within the Majority

If the Majority person is challenged because of his claim that the criminal is the product of society, he may feel safer by also *adding* genetics. If the capitalistic system turns out not to be an adequate explanation for the inept, unproductive employee, the Majority person can *add* heredity. If it seems too difficult to blame the failure of the flunking student upon the school system, his genes and chromosomes can be *added*. If it doesn't work to blame the parents of the misbehaving child completely, inborn factors can be *added*.

However, this combining of both heredity and environment sometimes seems to be embarrassing for the Majority. The result is often an even greater attempt to eliminate, more willfully, obviously and defensively, the whole concept of choice, learning, accountability, responsibility, etc. The extremity of this position and the difficulty of defending it seems to produce a tense shrillness. How did it come to this state?

Freud and Others Lay the Foundation[1]

In the early part of the twentieth century, something new and different occurred. For the first time in history, buck-passing was not merely tolerated, but boldly proclaimed as a total philosophy of life. Psychoanalysis with Freud, Behaviorism with Watson and Skinner, Education with Dewey and Spock, and other disciplines such as Humanism, Social Psychology, Sociology, Behavioral Science, Social Science, Penology,[2] etc., made contributions to beliefs as to what "controlled" our choices. The effect of the Irresponsibleness movement was that people no longer had to feel sheepish or embarrassed about leaving out the third factor of Accountableness — by sticking dogmatically to heredity and/or environment.

This is not to attribute bad motives to these leaders. It is probable that their motives were admirable. And they did make contributions to the understanding of human behavior and emotions. So where do we in the Minority part company with the Majority?

The Majority believe (and here I agree) that two of the most destructive emotions in human beings are guilt and hostility. Much of their life work has been dedicated to eliminating or curtailing these two emotions.

They attempt to overcome guilt by adopting an approach based on a premise that the individual has nothing to do with determining his heredity and little or nothing to do with determining his early environment. Since there is no third factor, then he cannot be held responsible for what he has become or what he has done. If a person can accept this position, it does seem that it should help him get rid of his feelings of guilt.

By the same token, he has to recognize that no one else can help being the way he or she is either. This fact presumably helps the individual to overcome his hostility toward others.

This Irresponsibleness system did seem to work in the beginning. For the first generation or two, it did seem to curtail guilt and hostility. By the third or fourth generation, however, guilt and hostility seem to have increased. Why?

If people and things from the past and the present have caused an individual to be the way he is, including his miseries and his goofs, then his *hostility* toward those things is *increased* because of what has been done to *him* by *them.*

The corollary is that if he is part of the people and things that have caused others to be the way they are, including their sins and unhappiness, then his *guilt* has been *increased* because of what has been done to *them* by *him.*

So this sensational new philosophy of life proposed by the Irresponsibleness people, which institutionalized that old part of original sin of buck-passing, did not work after all. It only made matters worse. Any honest look at America today will reveal that both guilt and hostility have increased significantly.

The Reality of Choice

This Irresponsibleness Point of View has influenced modern-day penology, sociology, education, political science, etc.[3] We are all supposedly products of our *heredity,* our *parents,* what we have been *taught* and what has *happened* to us. On the surface, that concept may seem sensible and acceptable. A closer look reveals that it is obviously not true. We are a product of what we have *selected from* our heredity and environment and *selected from* what we have been taught and what has happened to us.

That *selection process* began the first day we refused to eat the oatmeal (or before). Each of us has been selecting and rejecting ever since. When your son or daughter blames you for the way he or she feels and acts, you can instantly nip that buck-passing in the bud by pointing out that if it were true, he or she would have the same value structure and behavior patterns you have — that he or she would vote as you do, enjoy going to church with you, choose friends like yours, etc.

Each individual is offered a buffet of value structures, from parents first of all, then teachers, friends, etc. At first the selection process depends primarily on whatever feels good. As time goes by, the self-image and other more sophisticated criteria influence the selection process. But by definition, choice involves making selections that depart from the influence of heredity and environment.

What Causes Us To Be the Way We Are?

The Majority have been so conditioned to think of choosing as being purely a chemical reaction to heredity or environment, that choice therefore seems unreal — so unreal that it is usually ignored. If they feel forced to discuss it, they may ridicule it, treat it as naive religiosity or at best argue against it emotionally, philosophically and "scientifically." Most often, it just doesn't seem to exist.

While leading a workshop of professionals in the behavioral sciences, I asked them to name the factors that determine the way we are. I wrote on the chalkboard each item they suggested. When we had finished, the list looked like this:

Environment	Schools	Hang-ups
Money	Laws	Sex
Habits	Heredity	Perceptions
What has happened	People	I.Q.
Parents	Appearances	Lifestyle
Etc.		

The chalkboard was filled, and *no one had mentioned:*

Initiative	Dedication	Determination
Independence	Imagination	Decreeing
Creativity	Individuality	Ingenuity
Will	Freedom	Picking
Choice	Differentiation	Opting
Decision	Discriminating	Acceptance
Selection	Ordinating	Electing
Making-up the mind	Assessment	Approval
Commitment	Judgment	Etc.

When I mentioned a few of these items, the people at first thought I was kidding or teasing. One of them responded to the word "choice" by asking, "But what *causes* a particular choice?"

If something causes a choice, then, of course, it is not a real choice. All the factors the workshop members listed can make it *harder* or *easier* to make a certain choice. If those factors *cause* or *control* the choice, then the choice becomes merely an outcome, a result, a consequence that is inevitable, and is therefore not a real selection, not a real decision, not a real choice.

Even though most of those people never did agree with me (or perhaps even understand the point), at least they began to take me seriously when I pointed out that by the word "choice," we do not necessarily mean an instantaneous, right-now selection or decision; it may be a habitual pattern based upon a long series of choices. Also, we do not necessarily mean a conscious, deliberate, willful selection; it may be semiconscious, or even subconscious.

I did insist, though, that choice was more than just a chemical reaction to one's background. Otherwise, how could God hold us accountable for our choices?

It's Not Too Late

If a choice today is sometimes an automatic, spontaneous manifestation of previous choices, then we are at least accountable for those previous choices. At this point some of the group accused me of "laying a guilt trip on people" in regard to their past choices. I pointed out that Irresponsibleness lays a greater guilt trip on people by blaming them for causing the problems of other people in their lives. They didn't like that idea.

They also accused me of being hostile toward people because of their bad choices. I replied that Irresponsibleness triggers even greater hostility toward the people and things that "caused" one's problems and unhappiness. No acceptance here either.

It seemed to soften the blow, however, when I pointed out that it is *not too late* to change one's choices. It is unlikely, however, that an individual will change his choices until he faces and accepts the fact of his primary and ultimate Responsibleness for his choices. Facing Accountableness for one's choices is not as threatening as holding others accountable for those choices.

The group and I did seem to have some meeting of the minds when I pointed out that at any given point in time, even right at this moment, there is a sense in which a person does seem powerless to feel or act otherwise than his conditioning permits.

I illustrated this point with hypnosis. Once you have accepted a certain suggestion from a stage hypnotist or a party hypnotist, there is a sense in which you are powerless to do otherwise. Thus, it looks on the surface as if you are not under your own control, but under his. Let's look at this more carefully.

First, you made a choice or a selection to put yourself in the hands of a hypnotist. You know that a stage hypnotist is interested primarily in the show he is putting on, not in your personal welfare.

Second, you chose to accept the suggestion from him. You could have rejected it. You will not accept a suggestion from a hypnotist that you do not choose to accept.

Third, even when the hypnotic suggestion remains as a post-hypnotic suggestion, you still have the ability to sit down quietly, close your eyes, relax and choose to eliminate any suggestion that has been given you by *replacing* it with a different one — that is, by choosing a substitute, an alternative, a preference, a replacement. All hypnosis is self-hypnosis. Suggestions are rejected the same way they are accepted.

A law court that understands the true nature of hypnosis will not accept as a defense that the accused committed a crime under hypnosis. It is different when there has been a change in the brain structure through surgery, drugs, injury, disease, etc., or when there are birth defects or brain damage of any sort.

The Threat of Choice

The new counselee often is threatened by the concept of his Responsibleness for feelings going on inside of him. That is, until he looks at the *alternatives.* The other option is that people, places, things, situations out there or back there *really are* controlling the feelings going on inside of him. This other alternative is more threatening, a more fearful pressure.[4]

Facing accountability for one's choices may seem threatening at first, but when a person understands that it is a prerequisite for changing his choices, it becomes inspiring, uplifting, liberating, joyful, freeing. This freedom is spoken of in Scripture, as in the following verses.

Freedom

"And you shall know the truth, and the truth shall make you free."

John 8:32

"Therefore if the Son makes you free, you shall be free indeed."

John 8:36

Stand fast therefore in the liberty by which Christ has made us free, and do not be entangled again with the yoke of bondage.

Galatians 5:1

Now the Lord is the Spirit; and where the Spirit of the Lord is, there is liberty.

2 Corinthians 3:17

He who looks into the perfect law of liberty and continues in it . . . will be blessed.

James 1:25

The Majority and Minority Approaches to Depression

Jennifer came to our office complaining of depression, one of the more common problems we deal with. The depression often grows out of the discomfort of seeing oneself as a victim, a helpless animal, who is being controlled by forces beyond one's power. Realizing that these attitudes are not valid is the key to a cure for some depression.

Jennifer had first gone to a different counselor. Many counselors I know have healthy and valid motivations; they are sincere people who truly want to help their clients. This Majority psychoanalyst first sympathized with Jennifer. He told her that she was not to blame for her depression, that she had more than her share of pressures, that she shouldn't feel guilty about her condition, and that he personally would probably feel a lot worse if he had been subjected to all the hardships that she had endured. He sat by her side, held her hand and comforted her because of what she had been "controlled" by.

This sympathy felt good to Jennifer. Here was someone who understood and cared. As much as Jennifer appreciated the sympathy however, she didn't get well. In fact, she got worse. The analyst encouraged her to seek "causes" from the realities or forces outside herself, beyond her control, from her background. This counseling only reinforced the depression.

If background factors such as heredity and/or environment are *causing* the depression, then of course the therapist cannot help the counselee get out from under their control. He cannot go back and change the heredity or the previous environment. It is unlikely that he can significantly change even the counselee's present environment — the only way would be by giving up his other clients and spending all his time with this one depressed person, changing those persons, places, things, situations, etc., that are causing the depression. Again, my response is: "Good luck!"

It is easy for Christians to be tempted by this sympathetic type of therapy. It seems so considerate, so kind, so caring, so loving, so affirming and compassionate.

But while the counselee enjoys and appreciates it, too often, like Jennifer, she doesn't get well.

Finally Jennifer came to us for psychotherapy. After expressing sincere Christian sympathy, we moved on into confronting Jennifer with her own Accountableness for her own emotions. When the typical Majority therapist finds out about our accountability approach, he criticizes us: "How cruel to lay that guilt trip on these poor, defenseless, depressed persons and blame them for their own feelings!" But Jennifer got well, and so do most of the others we counsel.

The approach that is cruel is the opposite — the Irresponsibleness approach that advocates the ducking of responsibility. In the long run the counselee feels worse and does not get well.

Dealing With Guilt

At a state mental hospital where I was working, a man had involutional melancholia. The major symptom was a guilty conscience. He kept babbling about his sins, washing his hands and fretting because God would not forgive him.

The Irresponsibleness-type psychiatrist who was working with him kept telling him: "You haven't really sinned. There is no such thing as sin. You can't help what you have done. You are simply a product of your heredity and environment, and you had nothing to say about them. You shouldn't blame yourself. Something beyond your control has caused you to be the way you are. Accept yourself, etc." The psychiatrist was able to help the man temporarily to eliminate some of the feelings of guilt, but at too great a price — by relinquishing his personal Responsibleness. And he didn't get well.

What would a Christian psychiatrist have told him? "Of course, you have sinned. Who hasn't? But God still loves you. He will forgive you. Confess your sins to Him, and then, He as your Father, you as His son, will work together to move ahead."

It is possible to deal with guilt without eliminating responsibility. This is an amazing value of Christianity. Jesus "laid guilt trips" on people, but He always accompanied them by the solution to them — confession, repentance and forgiveness. The agony of guilt needs to last but a moment. The joy of restoration goes on forever.

Guilt is not the bugaboo for Christians that it is for the Majority. It is true that guilt feelings may temporarily result from facing and accepting the fact of one's own ultimate and primary Accountableness for one's own responses. The Christian who understands his faith knows how to deal with his guilt. If it is valid guilt in response to things about which he should feel guilty, he knows to confess, repent and accept God's forgiveness, cleansing and restoration.

On the other hand, he also knows that it is wrong to feel guilty in response to things for which he is not responsible and over which he has no control. With the Lord's help he learns to quit feeling such inappropriate or invalid guilt.

One argument that some of the Majority use is that we should *not* hold people accountable for their emotions — excessive anger, depression, fear, lust, vengefulness, etc. They argue that if we criticize people for these emotional feelings, it will just add to their guilt. By that same argument, we should never criticize lying, stealing, cheating, gossip, adultery and perhaps even murder, because such criticism will make those who commit these acts feel guilty. The Bible puts as much emphasis on emotional sins, sins of the inner being, as it does upon sins of behavior — in fact, even more emphasis.

Whether emotional sins or behavioral sins, they do often just seem to happen, rather than being deliberately planned. Some can be natural responses. But the point is that *it's not too late*! You and I can choose to channel and manage them in the future, to increasingly implement that change, with God's grace.

In conclusion, we admit that the Accountableness approach has problems, but they are not as great as the problems of the Irresponsibility approach. The problems of both are intensified when applied to relationships. Let's look at why the Accountability approach still is more acceptable, even when relationships are involved — in fact, especially so.

Chapter 9
ACCOUNTABILITY IN RELATIONSHIPS

In a twelve-week class, we had talked much about happiness as a choice. One woman seemed to be resistant, but she had not said much. Finally, during the twelfth session, she blurted out, "That seems so selfish!" I asked her to explain. She said, "For twelve weeks we have talked about what I want for myself. It seems selfish to be so concerned about my happiness. In marriage, and some other relationships too, I ought to be concerned with what I can give, not what I can get."

What Is Unselfish?

Her statement was one of those half-truths which can be more misleading than no truth at all. The principle we are talking about is the most unselfish, generous, kind thing you can do for another person. When you accept the primary Responsibleness for your own inner harmony and happiness in your marriage, that lets your mate "off the hook." It relieves him or her of the impossible responsibility of making you happy — a responsibility your spouse knows intuitively he or she cannot fulfill. To hold yourself accountable rather than your mate is generous.

The woman still argued, "But the emphasis ought to be upon others, not upon me at all." No, this is not what the Bible teaches — we are to love others as *ourselves*. (Matt. 22:39.) I pointed out to her that if we are really concerned about others, the most healthy, helpful, constructive thing

121

we can do for them is to encourage them to face and accept the fact of their own Accountableness, ultimately and primarily, for their own responses, including their happiness — and to set an example for them by doing the same for ourselves.

For twelve weeks it had been difficult for her to see beyond her strong sentimental and humanistic upbringing. She had always believed that, for a married couple, the husband's job was to make his wife happy, and the wife's job was to make her husband happy. For weeks we had been contradicting her life's beliefs.

Sentimental Attempts To Go Beyond 49%

The majority of people in our culture have been influenced by nineteenth-century, sentimental novels, or by early, idealistic Hollywood movies.

"Marry me and I will give you happiness."

"They got married and lived happily ever after."

"I just want to make others happy."

These romantic views are the opposite of what they seem. If my job is to make others happy, the implication is that their job is to make me happy. How arrogant, supercilious, condescending and selfish! And how impossible!

The young romantic sees a married couple celebrating a wedding anniversary after many years of happiness. He is inclined to say, "Look at how they make each other happy." Such is not the case. Each can make it harder or easier for the other one to be happy — even up to 49% worth. The other still has the 51% controlling vote.

No one has ever made anyone else happy. Happiness is a "do-it-yourself" job — with God's empowering, of course. In a happy marriage, what has happened is that two individuals have accepted the Responsibleness for their own happiness, and with God's help have disciplined themselves to be happy; then they have joined together and shared that personal happiness with each other.

If two truly happy people come together to establish a close, ongoing relationship — whether marriage or any other — what will be the style and quality of that relationship?

If you think that a particular person can make you happy, you should run as fast as you can in the opposite direction and not enter into a relationship with that person. If that individual can make you happy, then he or she also has the power to withhold happiness from you; and, being the fallible human beings we are, he or she will do that very thing at times.

To hold another person accountable for your own happiness is the most selfish thing you can do.

Is It Possible To Steal a Person's Joy?

One of the most valuable possessions any human being has is his own inner joy. When a husband feels that his wife has robbed him of this precious possession, his inner joy, he will probably harbor hostility toward her. But when he knows that she has never been able to, and never will be able to rob him of this precious possession, his inner joy, any other hostilities he feels towards her will be possible to deal with.

Conversely, when he feels that he has robbed his wife of this precious possession, her inner joy, he will harbor guilt, unless he is a malicious sadist. When he knows that he never has done so, and never will, and does not even have the capability to rob his wife of this precious possession, her inner joy, any other things he feels guilty about (even making it harder for her) will be possible to deal with.

These achievements are made without sacrificing personal Accountableness — on the contrary, by building squarely on it — which is the opposite of the Irresponsibleness approach.

Thus when both mates, or any two people in a close, ongoing relationship, face and accept the fact of their own Accountableness, ultimately and primarily, for their inner experiences, emotions and responses, then the two major problems encountered in counseling — guilt and hostility — can be decreased.

Accountableness for Actions Also

This absence of accountability for the other person's emotions does not mean that we are not accountable for what we do and say to one other. The Bible says much about how we are to treat other people.

God holds us accountable for treating others well, but He also holds us accountable for constructive emotions in ourselves, even when others don't treat us well.

He holds others accountable for treating us well, but He does not hold them accountable for how we ultimately choose to respond emotionally.

He holds us accountable for teaching our children right, but He does not hold us accountable for *making* them choose to learn.

He holds us accountable for how we treat our employees, but He does not hold us accountable for *making* them respond properly.

As we have said before, this 49%-51% balance doesn't decrease our motivation to do good to the other person. It usually intensifies it, for four reasons. One, we see pleasing God as more realistic and possible. Two, the decrease of guilt and hostility is a liberating experience and frees us to do what is right. Three, the unique experience of doing good toward others for the proper motivation — just because it's right, not to make the person happy — frees us from stress and guilt. We know intuitively that such a task is impossible. It is therefore frustrating and produces tensions that interfere with our effectiveness. Four, knowing that *making* the other person happy is not our job helps us to accept the more realistic job of contributing to that end within our possible 49%.

If we take accountability for the responses of other people, usually they either tend to rebel against our attempt to control and manipulate or hold us accountable for their responses. In either case, they blame us for their miseries — perhaps for the rest of their life.

A Good or a Bad Childhood

Trying to make sure that children have a "good childhood" can be just as "manipulative" and "controlling" as giving them a "bad childhood." In our counseling, we literally have as many problems with those who had a good childhood as with those who had a bad childhood.

The grown-up child from a good childhood may either resent his parents' "manipulation," or else he may want, in a dependent way, to "go back" and not have to move on into independent maturity. He can become frustrated with people and things because they are "not as nice as they used to be" and refuse to deal with the hardships of adulthood. Often the person from a bad childhood is more ready to put such things behind him and move on to better things.

In a sense we all had a bad childhood, in that we had two human beings for parents. Many counselees try to justify their parents by insisting that their parents did the best they knew how. Of course, that's not really true. No parent does that — because they are all human beings.

When a person makes such a claim about his parents, he is often subconsciously trying to justify himself. He is telling himself that just as his parents did the best they knew how, he too is doing the best job of parenting he knows how — which, of course, is not true either, since he also is a fallible human being.

Why Relationship?

In our marriage counseling, after we have established the Accountableness Principle, the question invariably comes up: "If I am responsible for my own inner happiness, if my mate can neither make me happy nor take away my misery, then what is the point of being married? The 51% Principle seems to contradict the meaning and function of marriage."

Buford came to counseling to get me to justify his leaving his wife, Betty, so he could marry the woman he now "loved," Ruth. He finally issued the challenge: "Now let me get this straight. If all that you are saying is true, then my happiness does not depend on my staying with Betty." I admitted that was true. He felt that he had me trapped. "Then I may as well leave Betty and go with Ruth!" I agreed that as far as his own emotions were concerned, he may as well.

After Buford's surprise and pause, I added, "Now, let's look at it from the other side. By the same token, your happiness does not depend on Ruth. Therefore, you may as well stay with Betty."

"That's not very romantic," he sputtered. "You *may as well* leave, or you *may as well* stay."

I pointed out that, on the contrary, it was the most romantic concept of all. If I felt that my wife loved me and married me because of my irresistible charm, that she was a victim and couldn't help herself, I would be concerned that my charm might fade or someone else with more charm might come along. Such tension *interferes* with romance.

Commitment, Romance and Freud

The most romantic concept known to man is the one that says that *love is a choice.* Also it is the most biblical. The Apostle Paul commands: "Husbands, love your wives" (Eph. 5:25). Likewise, to one of his disciples he wrote: "Admonish the young women to love their husbands" (Titus 2:4).

I own the 51% of my emotions and therefore have the final control and Responsibleness for what is going on inside of me, my happiness, my love, etc.

To think that my wife *chose* to relate to me, that she *chose* to keep relating to me, *chose* to commit herself to continue to relate to me "till death do us part," *chose* to love me, *chose* to keep loving me, *chose* to commit to continue to love me "till death do us part" — that is romantic.

The frivolous way that people take marriage vows today, their cavalier attitude toward divorce, even living together without making a marriage commitment — all of this is not surprising in terms of several generations of the Majority concepts.

If people and things control our happiness, we would be a fool to make a commitment to anybody "for better or for worse till death do us part." From that Majority point of view, the only relationship that makes sense at all is, "We will stay together as long as we make each other happy. When you quit making me happy, then of course I should leave. When I quit making you happy, I would not expect you to stay."

Only when a person faces and accepts the fact of his own primary and ultimate Accountableness for his own responses does it make sense to make a commitment to stay in a relationship permanently. If an individual is not committed to a relationship, why cultivate his own love and joy? If he is committed to stay, why not?

It took several generations for the Irresponsibleness Theory to produce its outcome, but that consequence is not mysterious, nor should it have been unpredictable. The only offer that makes sense from that Majority Theory is: "Let's not make any commitments or vows, just take a crack at it for a while and stay as long as we *feel* good about it.

The Decision and Self-Discipline

To Buford, who said that he may as well leave Betty, my answer was that he may as well stay with Betty. His next question was a practical one: "Then how do I make the decision whether to leave or stay?" I asked how he would be better off financially, by leaving or staying? His response was, "By staying." I asked how he would be better off in terms of community, church and relationship with God? He said, "By staying." I asked how the families would feel better, and he answered, "By my staying." I asked how the children would be better, and he reasoned, "By my staying." Every issue that we could think of, he agreed would be better by his staying, including faithfulness to his vow, "till death do us part."

He finally concluded, "Well, I may as well stay. What is just as important, I may as well make my decision to be happy. And I may as well make the decision to love Betty, really love her romantically." Then we were ready to get to work on the cultivating, the learning, the discipline.

Not all of the tangible issues may be, in every case, valid reasons for staying, as they were for Buford. Nevertheless, the principles are still the same. It is a matter of staying regardless of the tangible issues. Having made the commitment to stay, it is also a matter of committing oneself to love and be happy regardless of the tangible issues. This concept is considered at length in another book of ours entitled *The Unearned Relationship: Relationship Therapy*.[1]

True Spontaneity Is Hard Work!

One young lady in one of my classes made a statement (a theoretical one since she wasn't married or even engaged) that if her husband had to *work* at loving her, she would divorce him. If her fiance had to *work* at loving her, she insisted, she would never marry him: "I don't want to have to *work* at it. Love is supposed to be spontaneous . . . like the flowers grow spontaneously."

I agreed that love is to be spontaneous, like the flowers grow spontaneously. But I added that if we want a beautiful garden, the flowers require planting, watering, fertilizing, protecting, pruning — much work.

She muttered that the flowers weren't a very good illustration after all. Yes, they are. Working at something is not in conflict with spontaneity. It is the way one produces the right kind of spontaneity. So it is with love and marriage and relationships in general. They are skills, and like other skills, are cultivated.

There apparently is such a thing as a natural-born athlete or a natural-born musician. Such an individual may star for awhile, just on natural ability and without much discipline. It is interesting how, in time, the disciplined person will often surpass him. The gifted one sometimes is baffled about what happened. By the time he figures it out, sometimes it is too late to catch up. The natural one can enjoy more spontaneous effectiveness at first, but in the long run the disciplined person can surpass him in spontaneous and "natural" effectiveness.

The Fallacy of "Divorce for the Children's Sake"

Buford, deciding to stay with Betty, had one last question — about the children. He did have some serious criticisms of his wife. If he had left, he had intended to try to get custody of the children. He felt that Betty was a harmful influence on them. He truly loved his children and was sincerely concerned about them.

I asked him if he would like to help his children learn the true secret of life. He replied that he would. I quoted him the passage from Paul in Philippians, Chapter 4, about learning to be content in any and every situation of life. I reminded him that the most important thing his children could learn is that their inner peace and happiness, and the overcoming of their harmful emotions, did not depend on anybody or anything outside themselves, even their parents.

I suggested that he might teach his children this principle in precept, but that it would perhaps be more effectively taught by example. The worse his wife got, the greater his opportunity to set an example of keeping his own inner peace anyhow.

Even when he failed to do so and did get upset, he could still be a good example by not blaming the children's mother for his own emotional turmoil.

Even when he did slip and blame Betty for his own tensions, sooner or later he could retract it, and thus could be the greatest influence of all on the children.

No matter how bad Betty was, or became, the situation only increased his opportunity to teach his children "the true secret of life."

Buford then asked the right question: "Then will you teach me how to cultivate the inner emotions that I choose — love, joy, emotional stability, etc. — and how to overcome destructive emotions?" He was rightly asking to leave theory and move into practice. It is this practice, the "how to," the "tools," that are discussed more in depth in another book of ours entitled *Goal Therapy*.[2]

Not Mysterious

What are the techniques for changing, or reinforcing or handling in any way one's inner emotions? Like most people, Buford had conceived of these questions as being in the realm of the mysterious. Let's use an analogy.

There was a time when sailors got scurvy on long voyages. People saw something mysterious in this situation, even suggesting that evil spirits came up out of the ocean to attack the seamen. Finally they learned that scurvy was caused by a lack of Vitamin C, which, being unstable after weeks at sea, became insufficient. Once they learned how to preserve Vitamin C, there was no more scurvy!

Most people no longer see the principles of nutrition as mysterious. They understand that it is a scientific matter that operates by laws — laws of vitamins, minerals, proteins, etc.

The Christian knows that God made our food and the laws that govern it, made our minds capable of understanding them, made our bodies capable of utilizing them, made our wills capable of disciplining ourselves in applying them and made our spirits able to see the ultimate meaning and value of these laws as they apply to all of life, even to eternal significance.

Nevertheless, the laws of emotional nutrition are still seen even by some Christians as mysterious, in the manner that people formerly saw physical nutrition as mysterious. The laws of emotional nutrition are as specific, tangible and scientific as the laws of physical nutrition. As Christians we know that God made them and expects us to study and discipline ourselves in applying them.

The Learning of Accountableness in Relationship

In the case of Buford's remaining married to Betty, the result of the counseling was successful. In other cases, when a person is convinced that his real problem is his mate and is not willing to change such a mindset, we usually cannot prevent divorce. In the years that we have been counseling, we have not recommended divorce, because the Bible says that God hates it. (Mal. 2:16.) But we cannot always prevent it, when the counselee refuses to give up, even for a trial period, the Irresponsibleness Theory.

We do better in helping to save second marriages than first ones. When a person comes in during his second marriage and has the same complaints that he had in his first, it doesn't take a high I.Q. for him to suspect that the problem may be with himself, as much as, or even more than, with his mate.

Our counseling doesn't always succeed even there. One man wanted us to approve his getting a divorce from his seventh wife because now he had finally met the woman who was going to make him happy. None of the previous seven had made him happy, but this one would!

The book of Proverbs warns several times about the "strange woman." The term has significant meaning, but commentators differ on what that meaning is. I am inclined to think it is this shadowy figure in the back of a man's mind, a figure who is the ideal, the one who will make him happy. The theory that there is "that one right person for me" can be dangerous, if we mean the one who will make us happy. Then whenever we are unhappy, there is always the question of whether we did choose the right one.

Why Divorce?

One woman came in for counseling, complaining vigorously about her husband. Probably many of her complaints about him were valid, but her own inner miseries were her problem.

Two of her friends were encouraging her to "dump the bum." They saw him as making her miserable, and therefore to them divorce was the only answer. I was not able to convince her otherwise.

She got the divorce, and for several months she was much more relaxed and cheerful. Her two friends considered this change to be proof that they had been right and I had been wrong. The friends insisted that she had done the right thing, and that she was her old happy self again, which supposedly proved that her husband had been the cause of her unhappiness.

She continued to come in for counseling. About six months later, without seeing any connection, she began to make the same criticisms about her boss that she had made about her husband some months earlier. She acknowledged that she was beginning to experience some of the same old tensions.

If a person leaves or stays with a marriage or any relationship, for reasons listed on the double-columned sheet in Chapter 2, thinking that leaving or staying will add to his happiness or curtail his miseries, then it will be an unsatisfying decision. If he makes such a decision for any reason on the double-columned sheet, he will be disappointed in the long run. Unless the decision is made solely for ethical, legal, moral or safety reasons, he will continue to be unhappy.

Yet this advice is what the Majority gives, including the majority of counselors: "If any relationship is not making you happy, or is making you miserable, you should leave it." After several generations of Irresponsibleness brainwashing, this answer is seen as the right one, without question. No other alternative is conceivable to some people.

But the Bible says differently: "There is a way that seems right to a man, but its end is the way of death" (Prov. 14:12; 16:25).

One difficulty keeps arising, even with sincere people: "It is hard not to blame others." In all of my counseling over the years, the question I have asked more than any other in response to this statement is: "*As compared to what alternative?*" Yes, it may be hard not to blame others, but as compared to what alternative? It is harder *to* place the blame on others, because it makes us victims. As painful, threatening and difficult as it may be to face the fact of our own ultimate and primary accountability for our emotional responses, to hold others accountable for our emotions is worse, at least in the long run.

The "Barrier"

A more subtle form of buck-passing is projecting accountability not to some other *person* but to some supposed *"barrier"* out there "between" the partners. The fear, the depression, the anger, etc., is blamed not on the other person but upon "the barrier." It is the barrier that supposedly breaks down communication: "There is tension between us."

The only thing *between* any two people is oxygen, nitrogen and carbon dioxide — that is, air. The tension is not "out there" in space. It is inside the skin of one or both of the two people. We could measure the intensity of it in each with biofeedback instruments. We could not measure any tension in the air between them. The tension that is inside my skin is primarily my job to work on. The tension that is inside the other person's skin is primarily his job to work on. We might help each other, but never more than 49%.

Ways of avoiding facing Accountableness individually are numerous. Here is a list of some we have heard. These are usually given as reasons for getting a divorce.

Invalid Reasons Given for Divorce

1. "This marriage isn't going anywhere."
2. "This marriage isn't working out."

3. "We are making each other miserable."

4. "We are not good for each other."

5. "We can't love each other."

6. "Neither one of us has the courage to leave."

7. "We each need to do what's good for us."

8. "We're not nurturing each other."

9. "We will be better off separated."

10. "The circumstances are not conducive to our relationship."

11. "Communication has broken down."

12. "We are destroying each other."

13. "Our relationship is out of control."

(Compare this last one with a newspaper report after an accident stating, "The car went out of control." The car was never *in* control. It was the person who went out of control, not the car. Similarly, the "relationship" is not what's out of control, it's the people in the relationship.)

All of these are weaseling, buck-passing "cop outs."

One man in class said, "What if two people are destroying each other in marriage? Surely God would not expect them to stay together."

I answered, "If she's destroying you, don't let her. If you're destroying her, quit it."

He gulped, but as a Christian, he knew that was the right answer.

The 49% in Relationship

Whatever influence the other person may be having or failing to have on your emotions is his 49% or less. This maximum 49% may make it harder for you to respond in certain ways. You still own your 51%, however, and have the final Accountableness for the responses you choose and cultivate. God holds the other person accountable for how he treats you, but God holds you accountable for how you respond.

By the same token, with your 49% you may have a powerful influence on the responses of the other person. You may make it harder or easier for him to respond in certain ways. God holds you accountable for how you treat the other person, but God holds the other person accountable for the responses he chooses and cultivates.

The most Christian attitude you can have toward others, and maybe even occasionally state out loud, is: "I'm not the cause of your miseries. When I do bad things, I commit myself to asking God's forgiveness and yours. However, I choose not to feel guilty about your responses. To do so would be the most potentially destructive thing I could say or do to you. To the degree that you hold me responsible for your responses, you are forfeiting the true secret of life — your Accountableness for your own responses."

Ask yourself the ultimate question about relationship, especially the closest relationship of all, marriage: Why does God insist on "for better or for worse, till death do us part?"

If we do not have the 51% ownership of our own emotional responses, God's policy is the ultimate cruelty. It is only when an individual faces and accepts the fact of his primary and ultimate Accountableness for his own responses that he can possibly maintain belief both in God's love and God's admonition of unconditional permanence in marriage.

Marrying for the "Wrong" Reasons

In our counseling, we often hear the lament, "I got married for the wrong reasons." Let's examine this reasoning to see if it is truly valid.

Sally had a list of what she wanted in a husband, and Sam seemed to match her list. But she realizes now, she says, that she "didn't really love him."

Paradoxically, we get the opposite lament from Margie. She married George because she "fell in love with him" and he "fell in love with her." Now she thinks she should have been more objective about the list of "practical" issues involved with choosing a mate.

Both feel they got married for the wrong reasons even though those reasons are what the other partner considered to be the right reasons. And they both did marry for the wrong reasons. The practical attributes on the list will change unless they are maintained by commitment and discipline. But so will the love one "falls into" fade unless it is maintained by cultivation.

It should be obvious that each of these reasons, by itself, is the wrong one. The reason they are each wrong is that the underlying assumption in each case is that the list, or the "love," is going to produce personal happiness.

What we tell both men and women is, "Marry a person who has made up his or her mind to be happy and who does not promise to make you happy." Then both the practical issues and the love itself will probably be cultivated by each partner and shared.

So we now face the limits of the influence we can exert on another human being. Since we never "own" more than 49% of any other person, let's look at the issue of settling for that.

Chapter 10
SETTLE FOR FORTY-NINE PERCENT

We have called it the Minority Theory, the Accountableness Theory, the 51% Principle, Option III (in addition to Option I, influence, and Option II, avoiding), the third factor (in addition to heredity and environment), obedience to God's Amazing Commands, the Responsibleness approach, etc.

Just as important as that 51% Principle is the 49% Principle or Option I, influence (from Chapter 2). If I own 51% of the stock of the "corporation" of me and cannot sell it, give it away or lose it (except by destruction of brain cells), then all the people and things from my past and present can never make up, even altogether, more than 49% ownership.

Control Contrasted With Influence

Neither you nor I ever get more than 49% ownership of anyone else. We may not get 49%; we may not even get 4.9%. The point is that we *never get more* than 49% except by destroying some of the brain cells of that other person.

No matter how much influence we may exert in another person's emotional life, we can never exercise control of it. The practical question then becomes not how can we *control* that other person, but how can we utilize our 49% maximum to raise the probabilities of *influencing* that other person? Be sure to see the differences between the two: influence and control.

If *you* are responsible for *your* feelings and behavior (if you have your 51%), then you have less capacity than one might think to manipulate *other* people, since they are responsible for their responses (they have their 51%). This does not mean that you can't exert some influence. But are you satisfied with the possibility of exerting some influence without trying to cross over the 49% line into manipulation or control? Let's take a serious look at possible influence (Option I) and settle for what we can get.

The Fiction of Control

Aristotle wrote the first systematic textbook on Option I, how to influence another person's attitude.[1] In the first two thousand years since then, many other books have been written about how to influence others. Some people have tried to find ways of going beyond influence to manipulation or control. Some of them have offered tools which may seem to work for the moment. But none of them has provided a way to truly take over the control of the inner emotional responses of others, to get more than 49%. What they have come up with are functional, workable ways to make better use of the 49% and raise the odds of influencing others.

In all of these studies, the tools boil down to suggestions, bargains and rules. These are the sum total of Option I. Many labels, subdivisions and structures have been proclaimed, but they all come down to these three. These methods are considered in depth in another one of our books titled *Influence Therapy*.[2]

We might also consider the difference between physical control and emotional control: we may be able to lock a person in or out of a physical area; we may be able to pick up his body and place it somewhere else; we may be able to control his environment in a way that prevents or causes certain physical action patterns. We need to see that control of the *physical* is different from influence of the *attitude,* so physical control will not be included in our discussion, realizing that it may exist as a last resort where necessary.

An example of this final possibility would be the Birdman of Alcatraz (Chapter 6) who was confined behind bars and his body restrained. His jailers, however, could not control his thinking, emotions or attitudes. The same could be said about the limited influence of Corrie ten Boom's Nazi captors over her inner emotions.

The point is that suggestions, bargains and rules do not give control, only influence.

I sometimes work with managers of companies. Some of them, who have not thought the principle through, feel that there must be some way of gaining control of the responses of their employees. I often have a struggle getting them to settle for managerial techniques that make the most effective use of their 49%. Only then are they ready to work diligently on suggestions, bargains and rules and to settle for influence rather than control.

When a parent, manager, teacher, sales supervisor or any other leader faces the fact, once and for all, that there is no way to get ultimate control of the emotional responses of another person, he usually becomes more patient, more clever and more creative in exercising whatever influence is possible. He also usually becomes more relaxed, but more effective. He probably prays more. He takes more seriously the possibilities of suggestions, bargains and rules.

Even professional people are not immune to this desire to get more than 49%. When doctors, dentists or other professionals decide to study hypnosis, sometimes the reason is because they think it is a way of getting control of others. When they learn that, even in the deepest hypnosis, the subject still has the ability to accept or reject any suggestion made to him by the hypnotist, their typical response is often one of disappointment: "Well, then, what good is hypnosis?" It isn't any good if they see it as a way of dominating the reactions of their clients. It still does not go beyond suggestions, bargains or rules.

Attempts To Gain Control

I conducted a seminar for parents in a church. We began with the 49%-51% Principle. For the first half hour, it was as if I were speaking a foreign language. The people did not comprehend what I was saying.

After I defined terms and discussed meanings, they finally understood logically, but still thought the principles were ridiculous. One mother tensely challenged: "You mean to tell me that I can't control the attitudes of my own children?"

After another half-hour of defining and discussing, most of the parents agreed that this idea was true, but that it was a "bad system." Since the parents were churchgoers, I could defend it by pointing out that it was the system God made, according to the Bible, and that God usually subjects Himself to this system which He made.

All agreed that God usually does allow us our free wills, our genuine choices, even when those choices are bad. He tells us what is right and wrong. He warns us about the consequences of each alternative. Then He allows us to make choices, even when they are wrong, and lets us live with the consequences.

God does not usually take away our ownership of our decisions nor therefore the final control of our responses or our attitudes. Even though He can do so by supernatural miraculous interventions (and sometimes does), He normally limits Himself to suggestions, bargains and rules.

The parents were now willing to admit that they had never had more than 49% ownership of the attitudes of their own children. In fact, they agreed that it probably never got anywhere near 49%, maybe more like 4.9%!

The specific percentage is not the point. Each individual has the majority ownership, and therefore the final control, of his own emotional feelings and responses. Therefore no one else ever gets the majority ownership or the final control of his attitudes. To attempt to get that ultimate control of someone else's attitudes is to try to be like God and perform a supernatural miracle. We simply do not have that capability. When we try, the other person involved usually feels either hostile about being controlled or that he has a right to take the Irresponsibleness position and blame us for his responses.

Eventually the parents started asking the practical questions about Option I: "If we never have the majority ownership and therefore never have the final control even of our own children's attitudes, can you teach us techniques to make effective use of whatever minority ownership and input we do have?"

Then we got into the real issues of child-rearing techniques and began to discuss specific suggestions, bargains and rules. Finally, regarding one technique, the same woman who had the problem about controlling the attitudes of her own children interrupted: "I understand that principle, and I have used it myself, but *sometimes that technique doesn't work!*"

By her own statement, she "blew" the whole hour of discussion up to that point. Of course, *that* technique sometimes does not work. If she finds a technique that always works, one that never fails, then she does have 51% ownership of that child's responses and she does have final control. When I explained this to her, she reverted to her insistence that there *must* be a way to control the attitudes of her own children. She refused to settle for suggestions, bargains and rules.

I kept a straight face and told her that there was one way to get the majority ownership and the final control of the attitudes of her own child. She looked so relieved, as if I had been holding out on her. With mock seriousness I said, "Take your child to a brain surgeon, and have him do what they call a frontal lobotomy. This chops away that part of the brain that exercises freedom, initiative, creativity and individuality, and then you can control his attitudes and emotions."

"You know that's not what I want," she sputtered.

"If you are not willing to settle for the 49%," I challenged her, "then don't raise children. Raise dogs or horses, because you may be able to get more than 49% ownership of their responses and the final control. They are products of only two factors, heredity and environment. There is no real third factor of choice in the human sense."

Many parents, and other people in positions of leadership, assume that if rules and consequences are the strongest of the three tools, then surely we can make a person obey a rule if we make the consequences dire enough. This is a fallacy. If we make that assumption, then every rule we establish will eventually have, as its punishment, the death penalty. Sometimes even that doesn't work.

This is the mistake dictators make. It seems for a while that, when the punishments are dire enough, the dictator gains control of his subjects' attitudes, not just their actions. Sooner or later, however, even if it takes another generation or two, individual freedom and accountability again rear their heads and overcome the dictator. We see Communism now on the defensive. Three generations of brainwashing have not stamped out the sense of individual choice and Responsibleness. (See Chapter 12.)

Attempting to control the attitudes of others is trying to outdo God. He is the only One who has the right and the ability to control. Even He normally respects our 51%, which He gave us by creating us in His image and likeness, with free will.

The 49% in Marriage

Let's look at a sample case. My wife and I have seen this scenario in counseling many times:

Sam and Sally have been married for twenty years. Sam is the typical male chauvinist, and Sally is the classical submissive housewife. They are both tense and unhappy. Sally is angry because she feels that she is being controlled. Sam is angry because he feels that sometimes he loses control. They have lived together without killing each other for twenty years, both agreeing on one point: Sam is basically in control of Sally. Since they have never been able to reconcile their differences, they come in for counseling.

When we get to the subject of suggestions, bargains and rules as the tools of the 49% Principle, which is Option I (influence), they both think it is silly. Sam thinks the tools of influence are silly because he knows intuitively that they do not give him control. Sally thinks they are silly because she feels that Sam is going beyond them, and that he would never settle for the 49% and the three tools of implementing it.

We make the first inroad with Sally, before Sam, because she is more determined for some kind of change. We get Sally to see that Sam has never had more than suggestions, bargains and rules. She finally sees that for twenty years, she has been *choosing* to accept most of his suggestions because they really haven't been so bad. She understands that for twenty years she has been *choosing* to agree to most of his bargains because she has gotten something out of it. She realizes that for twenty years she has *chosen* to abide by many of his rules because they have been functional and fair. Choosing to go along with Sam's suggestions, bargains and rules has thus been less unpleasant than any alternative.

Sally finally realizes that Sam never has been controlling her, is not now controlling her and never will control her. Control is a fiction. No one controls anyone. She has been *choosing* to go along with Sam's suggestions, bargains and rules, and she *can* choose *not* to. Sally realizes that she is in charge of her own responses.

Because she has been feeling somewhat rebellious, Sally's next reaction is, typically: "Well, I'll show him! I'll choose not to accept any of his suggestions. I'll choose not to agree to any of his bargains. I'll choose not to abide by any of his rules." These attitudes come out in private sessions with Sally when Sam isn't present.

Then Sally calms down and begins to *feel* the fact that she's not really being controlled. She knows that she can choose otherwise. She decides that choosing to continue to go along with the suggestions, bargains and rules, even though there will be some painful moments, is not as painful in the long run as hostile rebellion.

Even if things are not fair, she may still be willing to live with a certain amount of unfairness, if it is the "lesser of two evils." She may not be able to exercise Option I and change Sam or the situation. Option II, leaving, may be worse for her, all things considered. There is no fourth option. All she has left is Option III, to change her own reactions. Even though it may not be fair, it is interesting how much we can stand with peace of mind when, as bad as it may be, we truly see the situation as preferable to the alternatives.

To Sally, the key is knowing that she is not being controlled, that she really does have her 51% ownership and that the final choice of how she feels and responds is hers. She chooses and learns to get over her anger and be a happier person. She no longer has a feeling of weakness.

Instead, she has a sense of emotional strength and stability, of being in charge and in control of her own emotional responses and resulting behavior.

Meanwhile, Sam is getting worse. He knows that Sally is no longer angry, tense, rebellious or resistant. Paradoxically, he feels that he is "losing control." She is not *doing* anything different, but he senses that she knows that it is she who is making the choices.

Sam blames us: "You're not helping me! You're not helping me get back my control! You're taking away my control!" Yet when we question him, privately, he cannot put his finger on anything that Sally is doing differently, except that she's not angry. Sam has been getting part of his "jollies" out of trying to manipulate Sally, and Sally no longer feels manipulated. Manipulation is in the eye of the beholder, at least in regard to attitudes. No one is being manipulated or controlled, or feels so, when he knows he is making the choices.

We wait for a session in which we can catch Sam in a mellow mood. We lay it on the line: "You never did control Sally, Sam. You cannot control her. No one ever controls anyone else, at least not their attitudes. All one gets are suggestions, bargains and rules, which you think are silly. The reason you think they are silly is because you know intuitively that they do not give you control. Give up the quest for control. Settle for the three tools of influence. Sally has been choosing to go along with your suggestions, bargains and rules, and she is probably going to continue to do so. Why do you want more than that? Settle for 49%. That better be enough, because that's all you're ever going to get." As we mentioned, this concept is developed in depth in our book *Influence Therapy*.

Sally is patient a little while longer. We get Sam to see that he has not lost anything, except "control," which he never had to begin with, and he has gained a lot. The one he loves has found peace of mind, and so can he. He has learned the tools of influence that apply to relationship. He and his wife have laid the foundation for a pleasant and productive relationship instead of a tense one. The key is his giving up the quest for control.

In fairness to Sam, Sally also has been trying to control in her own way. This was part of what Sam was angry about. The person who plays the "knuckle-under," "doormat" role is also attempting to control. Knuckling under, as painful and unpleasant as it may be, is a way of getting the other person off one's back, and in that sense is "controlling." Sam knew, subconsciously and intuitively, that Sally was gritting her teeth and going along with his suggestions, bargains and rules to keep him in his place. He had some resentment in this position.

Whence the Quest for Control?

Why this intense craving for control? The basic answer is simple.

It is the Majority Theory of Irresponsibleness, that people and things and background control our responses. We supposedly are not in charge of our responses, we do not possess the 51% ownership, we do not have Option III (in addition to Option I of influence or Option II of leaving), we do not have a third factor beyond heredity and environment, we do not have accountability for obeying God's commands about our responses, inner as well as outer.

If we are not in control of our responses, then neither are others in control of their responses. If somebody or something else is controlling *our* responses, then *we* can have a part in controlling the responses of *others*. The desire and attempt to control is a direct outgrowth and result of the Majority Theory, the Irresponsibleness approach, the abdication of accountability for our own responses. "If others are going to control my responses, then I am going to control theirs."

The Issue of Control in Adam and Eve

In addition to the psychological reason for the need to control, there is also a theological one. In Genesis, Chapters 1 and 2, Adam had control of what was outside of him and also what was inside of him. God held Adam accountable for his own inner responses, and also for the Garden of Eden. Adam was in control of the plants and the animals and all of his environment. He was also in control of his own inner responses, attitudes and feelings. God made it plain how Adam was to behave outwardly and inwardly. He was in control of things outside his skin and of things inside his skin.

Then Adam and Eve sinned. As a consequence, God took away one of the two areas of control — the things *outside* their skin. Adam and Eve were evicted from the garden. An angel with a sword was posted at the gate to keep them out. This action is an important symbol for us. There were no weeds in the original Garden of Eden. Weeds for us today are still an important symbol of a result of sin — God taking away from us the control of our environment.

However, God did not take away Adam's control of what was inside of him. After the Fall, God still held Adam every bit as accountable for his attitudes, beliefs, feelings, emotions, etc., even though Adam had less accountability for what was outside of him. God also promised that His grace would enable Adam to handle well that responsibility for his own inner responses. All of this perspective is set forth in the first three chapters of the Bible, Genesis, Chapters 1 through 3.

The Present Result

Because the Majority today does not understand the grace of God within us that enables us to maintain good control of our responses, they typically feel that they are actually *not in* control of what's inside of them. Even some Christians seem to fall into this trap. The lack of understanding of God's grace has helped give rise to the Majority Theory.

The Irresponsibleness approach makes an interesting point — most people are not doing a very good job of handling and controlling their inner responses. They therefore feel that they are not in charge, that somebody or something else is in control. Therefore, the idea that God holds us accountable for our own emotions is unthinkable to the Majority.

People still know intuitively that they are supposed to control something. Since they feel, erroneously, that they are not in control of what's inside of them, they feel strongly that they must control what's outside of them. Hence the attempt to control people and things around them. Again my response is: "Good luck!" God took away that power eons ago. He is apparently not going to restore it until the Millennium.

Many leaders feel that they are supposed to control the persons under their leadership — that it is their duty, their obligation. Yet probably, most people know intuitively that they cannot really control anyone else. There can be great frustration in leaders until they face and accept the 49% Principle.

Occasionally in our training programs the executives get upset with us because they expect us to teach their managers how to *control* the attitudes of their employees. It is difficult even to teach them the principles of *influence* of attitudes until they give up the quest for control.

While it is important for me to face and accept the fact of my own primary and ultimate Accountableness for my own inner responses — it is every bit as important for me to realize that I cannot and must not try to accept accountability for another person's responses.

Settling for the 49% Principle can come as a relief to leaders, and of course to everyone. What a relief not to *have to* control my spouse, children, employees, co-workers, boss, fellow church members, grandchildren, parents, brothers and sisters, clients, students, committee members!

If I believe that God chooses for me to use the three tools of influence to try to help others, it feels good. And of course, I can always pray for them. To go beyond the tools and prayer to the point of trying to control — what a denial of God's program and power!

Chapter 11
OBEDIENCE TO GOD IN EMOTIONS AS WELL AS BEHAVIOR: A SUMMARY

At this point, you don't have to decide whether you *believe* the main principle of this book — that emotions as well as behavior are an act of obedience or disobedience to God. But would you be willing to *operate* on this Minority Theory for a while?

If emotions are controlled by somebody or something else in the past or present (as most people believe), then you are doomed to a lifetime of being a victim of these outside influences. The only way to freedom is by facing and accepting the fact of your own ultimate and primary accountability for your own emotions — no matter how much harder it is made for you by anybody or anything in your past or present.

So the only way we can be of any help to you is if you tentatively and temporarily allow us to operate on the theory of Accountableness.

Willingness

Willingness is the key. Would you be *willing* to obey God in your emotions, if you could, with His help?

After a few sessions of counseling, one wife claimed several times, "I *can't* love my husband any more! I *have* to get a divorce." We finally asked, "If God made it possible for you to love him again, would you be *willing* to do so?" She burst into tears, ran out of the room, and we never saw her again. The husband later verified that this question was the right one. She simply was not *willing* to obey God and to accept His enabling grace to love him.

A question we like to ask a counselee is, "Would you be willing to do anything God asked you to do?" Sometimes we get the answer, "Well, I'd have to know what it was first." That's the wrong answer! Willingness *precedes* knowledge, not the other way around: "If anyone *wants* ["*will*" — KJV; "*chooses*" — NIV] to do His will, he shall *know* concerning the doctrine" (John 7:17). To know what is God's will is important, but sometimes this knowledge doesn't appear until after the willingness to do it, whatever it might turn out to be, is present first.

The True Secret of Life

Many of our counselees want somebody or something to make them happy, but they also want to quit being depressed. They don't realize that these two objectives are incompatible.

If other people could make us happy, then they could also withhold happiness from us. And being human, they would sometimes withhold our happiness.

If anything in the world had the power to make us happy, then it would also have the power to withhold happiness from us. The world, being under a curse (Gen. 3:17,18), would sometimes withhold our happiness.

We have quoted Paul the apostle, Samuel Johnson and others several times in this book in regard to "the true secret of life." As long as we depend on anybody or anything to make us happy and to overcome our miseries for us, we don't have a chance of finding happiness or overcoming our unhappiness. But wait! It gets worse! As long as we depend on anybody or anything, we not only fail to find happiness — we get more and more miserable as time goes by.

Happiness Is Not a By-Product

The common cliché that happiness is a by-product is the most weaseling, buck-passing "cop out" of all! Emotional feelings, including happiness, are a choice, an act of the will, a decision, a selection, a making up of one's mind — followed by an implementation of that choice through an ongoing, personal self-discipline of practice, repetition, drill and cultivation. All this requires God's empowering.

These activities are what *learning is*: The two common denominators of *all* learning are choice and cultivation, or selection and repetition, or decision and discipline, or an act of the will and then practice, or a making up the mind and then drilling over and over.

How do you apply these two components of learning to your own emotions? We might put the first of the two essentials into five steps:

1. When you are anxious and not joyful, quote to yourself Philippians 4:11-13: "Not that I speak in regard to need, for I have learned in whatever state I am, to be content: I know how to be abased, and I know how to abound. Everywhere and in all things I have learned both to be full and to be hungry, both to abound and to suffer need. I can do all things through Christ who strengthens me."

Memorize these verses, or at least type them out on a card and carry them around with you in your purse or pocket. Say them out loud if no one is around, or silently to yourself — whenever you are anxious or unhappy.

2. Also quote verse 6, "Be *anxious* for nothing" and verse 4, "*Rejoice* in the Lord always. Again I will say, rejoice!"

3. Say to yourself: "By God's grace I have the *ability* to learn to quit disobeying Him — to quit being anxious — and I can cultivate the *ability* to obey Him — to rejoice."

4. Say to yourself: "By God's grace I am *willing* to learn to quit disobeying Him — to quit being anxious — and I am *willing* to learn to obey Him — to rejoice."

5. Say to yourself: "By God's grace I hereby *do choose* to quit being anxious, and *do choose* to rejoice and to take the time and energy necessary to implement those choices."

Sometimes these five steps don't work immediately. *Sometimes they do!* Either way, then comes the second component of learning, the repetition, the cultivation.

If you stick with this commitment to obey in your emotions, again and again, the times that these steps work will come more often and more thoroughly — and more quickly and more easily. You are in your process of learning obedience to God in your emotions — through choice and cultivation — by God's grace and power and enablement.

As you progress, more and more you will quit believing Satan's lie that your emotions are being controlled by people, things and circumstances (even if it sometimes still *seems* that way). Your response is similar to the way people learned to quit believing the falsehoods that the earth was flat or that the sun rises and sets (even though it still *looks* as if the world is flat and the sun rises and sets).

Now we know that the earth is round, though it appears flat to us, and that as it rotates it gives the appearance of the sun rising and setting. Similarly, with God's enlightenment we can believe, yes, know, that in spite of the way it may seem to us at the moment, we *are* choosing and learning our emotions.

If we then try to do a better job of controlling our emotions, we get convicted of the difficulty, the impossibility, of doing so without God's help. We rely on Him in a deeper way. As we progress, we increasingly believe God's truth that emotions are an act of obedience or disobedience to Him.

As a final summary let's review the seven themes of this book:

1. Emotions, as well as actions, are an act of obedience or disobedience to God.

2. We are accountable for our emotions, as well as for our actions.

3. Emotions, as well as actions, have moral content.

4. It takes God's help to control emotions well, as with actions.

5. Emotions, like actions, are chosen and learned.

6. Background factors can make it harder or easier to experience certain emotions, as well as to perform certain actions.

7. Emotions take priority over actions.

Chapter 12
EPILOGUE FOR OPTIMISM: THE FALL OF COMMUNISM

The current failure of Communism was bound to happen. It cuts too sharply across basic human drives. The sense of accountability for one's own choice of responses is too deeply ingrained in the human breast.

It was not only Communism that tried to overcome this drive. Freudianism, Behaviorism, Nazism and to some extent naturalistic Humanism and atheistic Existentialism have all tried and have failed to do so. Therefore, as a viable human philosophy, none of these has worked. Whether one takes the Bible seriously or not, it does offer an explanation for this innate sense of accountability for one's choice of responses.

Since Adam and Eve chose to disobey God, humans no longer have complete control over their environment. Humans intuitively feel that they are supposed to control something. They go about trying to change and control those outside factors that they see as "causing" their inside response, rather than working directly with their own responses.

Freudianism tried to escape accountability for one's own responses by projecting it onto one's mother, or a bad childhood, or a traumatic event, etc. It failed.

Behaviorism tried to shift accountability to one's environmental conditioning and has failed.

Nazism tried to allow the state to assume accountability for its citizens. At the Nuremburg trials, the defense of each

Nazi was, "I was just obeying orders" — shifting account-ability from the individual to the state. Nazism has failed.

Humanistic social welfare made the shift by proposing methods by which we can make our environment right again. Such attempt to restore the perfection of the Garden of Eden is failing.

In Communism, the state also tried to take away its citizens' sense of accountability. Now we can see the outcome of that experiment. Dictatorships attempt to take away individual responsibility for personal responses. They sometimes seem to succeed for a time. But not indefinitely.

All of these attempts are efforts to overcome something that is too basic to be overcome — an intuitive sense of individual accountability and responsibility based on personal freedom, reality of choice, independence, creativity, imagination, initiative, etc. When a system fails to accomplish the take-over of accountability and the personal freedom that accompanies that accountability, the last resort is brute force, which is only physical control.

On the other hand, people sometimes are temporarily willing to allow a system to assume their accountability. They are willing to pay the price of their loss of freedom for the privilege of buck-passing on responsibility. Only temporarily does this action succeed, because sooner or later they end up feeling like victims — as though somebody or something is controlling them.

The other alternative, of facing and accepting the fact of one's own accountability for one's own responses, may be uncomfortable at first. But eventually accepting it is the only approach that gives true freedom. As attractive as blaming others may be, for most people it is not ultimately as attractive as freedom.

Communism was never the belief of most people. Some simply couldn't physically escape living under the system.

Once there was a weakening of the Communist leadership, the majority of people came out to rally against it. How dramatically we see this happening, with the people of Eastern Europe overthrowing Communism.

Some other people were sucked into the system because they found attractive the thought of escaping personal accountability. They realized too late that it was inescapable.

Still others tried hard to believe in the system. Their difficulty is revealed in their tenseness, defensiveness and shrillness as they still attempt to control the outside rather than the inside. Consider how shrill the cries of the Communist have been in recent years.

We are now seeing Communism crumble — for the very same reasons we are now seeing the crumbling of modern secular humanistic psychology, especially of the Freudian and Behavioristic types.

The dominant mood for a replacement is up for grabs. The biblical approach of facing and accepting the fact of one's own primary and ultimate accountability for one's own responses is an idea whose time has come again.

Appendix A
CHRIST IN YOU: THE KEY

"He who eats My flesh and drinks My blood abides in Me, and I in him."

John 6:56

"You will know that I am in My Father, and you in Me, and I in you."

John 14:20

"Abide in Me, and I in you."

John 15:4

"[I pray] for those who will believe in Me. . . . as You, Father, are in Me. . . . I in them. . . . I in them."

John 17:20,21-23,26

And if Christ is in you, the body is dead because of sin, but the Spirit is life because of righteousness. But if the Spirit of Him who raised Jesus from the dead dwells in you, He who raised Christ from the dead will also give life to your mortal bodies through His spirit who dwells in you.

Romans 8:10,11

But he who is joined to the Lord is one spirit with Him. . . . your body is the temple of the Holy Spirit who is in you.

1 Corinthians 6:17,19

Christ speaking in me . . . is not weak toward you, but mighty in you.

2 Corinthians 13:3

Do you not know yourselves, that Jesus Christ is in you?

2 Corinthians 13:5

"Christ lives in me; and the life which I now live in the flesh I live by faith in the Son of God, who loved me and gave Himself for me."

Galatians 2:20

Christ is formed in you.

Galatians 4:19

[I pray God for you] to be strengthened with might through His Spirit in the inner man, that Christ may dwell in your hearts through faith. . . . that you may be filled with all the fullness of God.

Ephesians 3:16,17,19

[God has revealed] the mystery which has been hidden from ages and from generations, but now has been revealed to His saints. To them God willed to make known what are the riches of the glory of this mystery among the Gentiles: which is Christ in you, the hope of glory.

Colossians 1:26,27

Christ . . . is our life.

Colossians 3:4

He who is in you is greater than he who is in the world.

1 John 4:4

By this we know that we abide in Him, and He in us, because He has given us of His Spirit.

1 John 4:13

"Behold, I stand at the door and knock. If anyone hears My voice and opens the door, I will come in to him and dine with him, and he with Me."

Revelation 3:20

Appendix B
THE POWER SOURCE: GOD

"You shall remember the Lord your God, for it is He who gives you power to get wealth."

Deuteronomy 8:18

"O Lord.... Both riches and honor come from You.... In your hand it is to make great and to give strength to all.... For all things come from You."

1 Chronicles 29:11,12,14

"If He should gather to Himself His Spirit and His breath, all flesh would perish together, and man would return to dust."

Job 34:14,15

"Without Me you can do nothing."

John 15:5

"In Him we live and move and have our being."

Acts 17:28

No human being might boast in the presence of God. He is the source of . . . our wisdom, our righteousness and sanctification and redemption.

1 Corinthians 1:29,30 RSV

What do you have that you did not receive? Now if you did indeed receive it, why do you glory as if you had not received it?

1 Corinthians 4:7

I labored . . . yet not I, but the grace of God which was with me.

1 Corinthians 15:10

Not that we are sufficient of ourselves to think of anything as being from ourselves, but our sufficiency is from God.

2 Corinthians 3:5

Now we live and are strong, as he is, and have all of God's power to use in dealing with you.

2 Corinthians 13:4 TLB

The God and Father of our Lord Jesus Christ . . . has blessed us with every spiritual blessing.

Ephesians 1:3

[God] is able to do exceedingly abundantly above all that we ask or think, according to the power that works in us.

Ephesians 3:20

It is God who works in you both to will and to do for His good pleasure.

Philippians 2:13

Every good gift and every perfect gift is from above, and comes down from the Father.

James 1:17

Appendix C
THE INNER BEING, THE HEART, THE ATTITUDES

"'I walk in the imagination of mine heart.'"
Deuteronomy 29:19

For the Lord seeth not as man seeth; for man looketh on the outward appearance, but the Lord looketh on the heart.
1 Samuel 16:7 KJV

"For the Lord searches all hearts and understands all the intent of the thoughts. . . . I know also, my God, that You test the heart and have pleasure in uprightness."
1 Chronicles 28:9; 29:17

Let the words of my mouth and the meditation of my heart be acceptable in Your sight, O Lord, my strength and my redeemer.
Psalm 19:14

If we had forgotten the name of our God, or stretched out our hands to a foreign god, would not God search this out? For He knows the secrets of the heart.
Psalm 44:20,21

Create in me a clean heart, O God, and renew a steadfast spirit within me.
Psalm 51:10

Keep your heart with all diligence, for out of it spring the issues of life.
Proverbs 4:23

A merry heart does good, like medicine, but a broken spirit dries the bones.

Proverbs 17:22

As he [a person] thinks in his heart, so is he.

Proverbs 23:7

"I will give you a new heart and put a new spirit within you; I will take the heart of stone out of your flesh and give you a heart of flesh. I will put My Spirit within you and cause you to walk in My statutes, and you will keep My judgments and do them."

Ezekiel 36:26,27

"Blessed are the pure in heart, for they shall see God."

Matthew 5:8

"For where your treasure is, there your heart will be also."

Matthew 6:21

"If therefore the light that is in you is darkness, how great is that darkness!"

Matthew 6:23

"But seek first the kingdom of God and His righteousness, and all these things shall be added to you."

Matthew 6:33

"Either make the tree good and its fruit good, or else make the tree bad and its fruit bad, for a tree is known by its fruit. Brood of vipers! How can you, being evil, speak good things? For out of the abundance of the heart the mouth speaks. A good man out of the good treasure of his heart brings forth good things, and an evil man out of the evil treasure brings forth evil things."

Matthew 12:33-35

"But those things which proceed out of the mouth come from the heart, and they defile a man."

Matthew 15:18

"Woe to you, scribes and Pharisees, hypocrites! For you cleanse the outside of the cup and dish, but inside they are full of extortion and self-indulgence. Blind Pharisee, first cleanse the inside of the cup and dish, that the outside of them may be clean also. Woe to you, scribes and Pharisees, hypocrites! For you are like whitewashed tombs which indeed appear beautiful outwardly, but inside are full of dead men's bones and all uncleanness."

Matthew 23:25-28

"From within, out of the heart of men, proceed evil thoughts. . . . All these evil things come from within."

Mark 7:21,23

"A good man out of the good treasure of his heart brings forth good; and an evil man out of the evil treasure of his heart brings forth evil. For out of the abundance of the heart his mouth speaks."

Luke 6:45

But he is a Jew who is one inwardly, and circumcision is that of the heart, in the Spirit, and not in the letter; whose praise is not from men but from God.

Romans 2:29

You obeyed from the heart.

Romans 6:17

For with the heart one believes to righteousness.

Romans 10:10

If the root is holy, so are the branches.

Romans 11:16

Be transformed by the renewing of your mind.

Romans 12:2

You are manifestly an epistle of Christ, ministered by us, written not with ink but by the Spirit of the living God, not on tablets of stone but on tablets of flesh, that is, of the heart.

2 Corinthians 3:3

For we do not commend ourselves again to you, but give you opportunity to glory on our behalf, that you may have something to answer those who glory in appearance and not in heart.

2 Corinthians 5:12

Be renewed in the spirit of your mind.

Ephesians 4:23

Be obedient. . . . doing the will of God from the heart.

Ephesians 6:5,6

Let this mind be in you which was also in Christ Jesus.

Philippians 2:5

Finally, brethren, whatever things are true, whatever things are noble, whatever things are just, whatever things are pure, whatever things are lovely, whatever things are of good report, if there is any virtue and if there is anything praiseworthy — meditate on these things.

Philippians 4:8

Set your mind ["affection" — KJV] on things above, not on things on the earth.

Colossians 3:2

Even so we speak, not as pleasing men, but God who tests our hearts.

1 Thessalonians 2:4

Do not let your beauty be that outward adorning of arranging the hair, of wearing gold, or of putting on fine apparel; but let it be the hidden person of the heart, with the incorruptible ornament of a gentle and quiet spirit, which is very precious in the sight of God.

1 Peter 3:3,4

Appendix D
QUOTATIONS ON INDIVIDUAL CHOICE AND RESPONSIBILITY

All the familiar goals in life are snatched away. What alone remains is the last of human freedoms — [the ability to choose] one's attitude in a given set of circumstances.

Dr. Viktor E. Frankl

The supreme good of man, according to the sages, lies in refining his act of judgment to the highest degree of purity, in learning to think properly, and in cultivating a good mind, since all our misfortunes are born of our inability to make the proper choices. . . .

Jean Guitton
Sorbonne professor of philosophy

Man alone, of all the creatures of earth, can change his own patterns. Man alone is architect of his destiny. The greatest revolution in our generation is the discovery that human beings by changing the inner attitudes of their minds can change the outer aspects of their lives.

William James

We forge the chains we wear in life.

Charles Dickens

Man is fully responsible for his nature and his choices. An individual chooses and makes himself.

Jean-Paul Sartre

Man must cease attributing his problems to his environment, and learn again to exercise his will — his personal responsibility in the realm of faith and morals.

Albert Schweitzer

. . . The patient cannot evade responsibility. Little good and much harm come from delving into the patient's history — the past cannot be changed or allowed to be used as an excuse for present irresponsibility. Morality and discipline have a definite place. . . .

O. Hobart Mowrer

Transactional Analysis . . . is realistic in that it confronts the patient with the fact that he is responsible for what happens in the future no matter what has happened in the past. Moreover, it is enabling persons to change, to establish self-control and self-direction, and to discover the reality of a freedom of choice. . . .

Freud and most behaviorists have held that the cause-and-effect phenomenon seen in all the universe also holds true for human beings, that whatever happens today can theoretically be understood in terms of what happened in the past. If a man today murders another man, we are accustomed by Freudian orientation to look into his past . . . that man's behavior is not free and is only a product of his past. The inevitable conclusion is that man is not responsible for what he does. . . .

Yet . . . human beings have become more than what they were. . . . Man has become more than his antecedents. . . . This is what is meant by self-causation as a genuine third possibility in our familiar dilemma.

Thomas A. Harris, M.D.
I'm OK — You're OK[1]

People do not act irresponsibly because they are ill, they are ill because they act irresponsibly. . . .

The therapist begins to insist that the patient face the reality of his behavior. He is no longer allowed to evade recognizing what he is doing or his responsibility for it. When the therapist takes this step — and he should start as soon as involvement begins — the relationship deepens because now someone cares enough about the patient to make him face a truth that he has spent his life trying to avoid: *he is responsible for his behavior.* . . .

The therapist who accepts excuses, ignores reality, or allows the patient to blame his present unhappiness on a parent or on an emotional disturbance can usually make his patient feel good temporarily at the price of evading responsibility. . .

In Reality Therapy, therefore, we rarely ask why. Our usual question is *What? What* are you doing — not *why* are you doing it? Why implies that the reasons for the patient's behavior make a difference in therapy, but they do not. The patient will himself search for reasons; but until he has become more responsible he will not be able to act differently, even when he knows why.

William Glasser, M.D.
Reality Therapy[2]

Slums have produced some of the nation's top business, professional and political leaders.

Some of Chicago's most useful citizens were born in the same neighborhood that spawned many gangsters.

. . . The rise in lawlessness suggests there is something wrong with our approach to the problem.

Certainly, in the development of good citizens no element is more important than a sense of individual responsibility.

> Vergil W. Peterson
> Operating Director
> Chicago Crime Commission

"Society doesn't cause crime. People cause crime."

This was the statement of Los Angeles Police Chief Thomas Reddin at recent graduation exercises for the FBI National Academy.

. . . This is tough talk that will horrify a number of departments of sociology. Because most of our gentle theorists are highly civilized people that cannot imagine criminal actions that are not compelled by forces over which the criminal has no control. They have, with the best intentions, supplied criminals with the holy rationale: "Look what you honest people did to me!"

. . . We have about played out the theory that American society should take the blame for the activities of criminals. The finely-spun theories that harshness to the wrongdoer must be replaced by efforts at social reform are in bankruptcy.

> Jenkin Lloyd Jones
> "First Order Is Order"
> *The Tulsa Tribune*
> January 5, 1968

Morality makes sense.

It also has a lot to do with mental health and happiness.

For a long time American psychiatry and the so-called "social sciences" have been preoccupied with

Freudian theories of suppressed sex drives and wounded libidos. From this it was often argued that people were really not responsible for anti-social behavior.

... Dr. Abraham Maslow has recognized that the effort to excuse the errant and to confront the unruly isn't paying off. He has laid down the following precepts:

Behavioral science which ignores moral decisions is grossly inadequate. . . . Man . . . usually has an innate bias in favor of freedom, justice and achievement.

There is a scientific basis for moral principles and it is rooted in human nature.

Dr. Harry Link, the clinical psychologist, says that, contrary to the Behaviorist theory that high moral standards mean repression, frustration, nervous illness and unhappiness, most people with high ideals are better adjusted to life than the swingers.

Another psychiatrist, Dr. Edward R. Pinckney, is bitter. "I hope," he has written, "that the world will return to the belief in love, ideals, good taste and courtesy — books that have been burned by the Freudian inquisition."

Dr. O. Hobart Mowrer, former president of the American Psychological Association, writes:

"We have good reason to believe that psychotherapy, instead of stemming from unexpressed sex and hostility, comes rather from an outraged conscience and a violated sense of human decency and responsibility."

Alcoholics Anonymous has a highly moralistic approach that wastes little time in worrying how the alcoholic became one or in clicking sympathetically over his plight.

. . . Synanon, the new program for drug addicts states: "We do not begin with a presumption of sickness, as has virtually all psychological orientation since Freud. Instead, we assume that people behave badly not because they are ill."

. . . Dr. Efren E. Ramirez who has had unusual success with addicts in Puerto Rico says: "The typical addict has a weak sense of responsibility, little commitment to anyone or anything."

"There comes a time when a man must stand up."

Maybe modern psychiatry is about to make that discovery, and we will quit coddling and cooing as our society slides toward chaos.

Jenkin Lloyd Jones
"On Standing Up"
The Tulsa Tribune
December 27, 1969

Appendix E
FINAL EXAM

Date _____

1. I HEREBY MAKE UP MY MIND TO BE HAPPY.

2. WHEN I SLIP AND BECOME UNHAPPY, I HEREBY MAKE UP MY MIND NOT TO BLAME MY UN-HAPPINESS ON ANYBODY OR ANYTHING.

3. WHEN I SLIP AND BLAME MY UNHAPPINESS ON ANYBODY OR ANYTHING, I HEREBY MAKE UP MY MIND TO QUIT DOING SO AS SOON AS I BECOME AWARE OF IT.

4. I UNDERSTAND THAT WHILE I MAKE THESE COMMITMENTS ONE AT A TIME, TODAY, I AM ABLE INCREASINGLY TO IMPLEMENT THEM ONLY AS A PROCESS, OVER TIME, BY THE GRACE OF GOD, IN MY ONENESS WITH CHRIST, BY THE POWER OF THE HOLY SPIRIT DWELLING IN MY PHYSICAL BODY.

5. WHEN I SLIP AND BECOME UNHAPPY, OR WHEN I SLIP AND BLAME MY UNHAPPINESS ON ANYBODY OR ANYTHING, I WILL NOT SEE THAT ACTION AS RENEGING ON MY COMMITMENTS. IN FACT, WHEN THE HOLY SPIRIT MAKES ME AWARE OF THE SLIP, I WILL ALLOW IT TO REMIND ME OF WHAT I AM REALLY COMMITTED TO AND THEREBY TO REINFORCE THE COMMITMENTS I HAVE MADE.

SIGNED _____

[2]William C. Lantz, Jr., Ph.D., *Goal Therapy* (unpublished manuscript).

Chapter 10

[1]Aristotle, *Rhetoric,* quoted in: Rhys Roberts, translator *The Great Books*, (Chicago: Encyclopedia Britannica, 1990).

[2]William C. Lantz, Jr. Ph.D., *Influence Therapy* (unpublished manuscript).

Appendices

[1]Thomas A. Harris, M.D., *I'm OK — You're OK* (New York: Harper & Row, 1967), pp. 24,86-88.

[2]William Glasser, M.D., *Reality Therapy* (New York: Harper & Row, 1965), pp. xv,xvii,27,30,32.

ENDNOTES

Introduction

¹James W. Newman, *Release Your Brakes!* (Thorofare, NJ: Charles B. Slack, Inc., 1977).

Chapter 1

¹A. J. Ungersma, *The Search for Meaning* (Philadelphia: The Westminster Press, MCMLXI), Chapter 2.

Chapter 2

¹William C. Lantz, Jr., Ph.D. *Goal Therapy* (unpublished manuscript).

Chapter 3

¹Donald F. Tweedie, Jr., *Logotherapy and the Christian Faith* (Grand Rapids: Baker Book House, 1961), Chapter 2.

²Barbara B. Brown, Ph.D., *New Mind New Body: Biofeedback: New Directions for the Mind* (New York: Harper & Row, 1974).

³Lee Birk, M.D., *Biofeedback: Behavioral Medicine* (New York: Grune & Stratton, 1973).

⁴Sigmund Freud, M.D., LL.D., *A General Introduction to Psychoanalysis* (Garden City, NY: Permabooks, 1935), Part I, Introduction, pp. 19,20.

⁵J. B. Watson, *Behaviorism*, Rev. Ed. (Chicago: University of Chicago Press, 1958).

⁶Norman Munn, L. Dodge Fernald, Jr., and Peter Fernald, *Basic Psychology* (Boston: Houghton Mifflin, 1972).

Chapter 5

¹Dennis Coon, *Introduction to Psychology: Exploration and Application* (St. Paul: West Publishing, 1977), pp. 459-466.

²Norman Munn, L. Dodge Fernald, Jr., and Peter Fernald, *Basic Psychology* (Boston: Houghton Mifflin, 1972), p. 65.

[3]Francis Schaeffer, *A Christian Manifesto*: Westchester, IL: Crossway Books, 1984), especially Chapter 3, "The Destruction of Faith and Freedom."

[4]Ella Wheeler Wilcox, "The Winds of Fate," quoted in: Al Bryant, compiler *Storehouse of Poetry* (Grand Rapids: Zondervan Publishing House, 1979), p. 73.

[5]William Barclay, *The Letters to the Philippians, Colossians and Thessalonians*, one volume of *The Daily Study Bible* (Philadelphia: The Westminster Press, 1959), pp. 103,105.

[6]Gerald Hawthorne, *Word Biblical Commentary*, Vol. 43 (Waco: Word Books, 1982), p. 200.

[7]Robert W. Wicks, *The Interpreter's Bible*, Vol. XI: *Exposition of Philippians* (New York: Abingdon Press, 1955), p. 122.

[8]Walter Bauer, *A Greek-English Lexicon of the New Testament*, 2nd Ed. (Chicago: University of Chicago Press, 1979), p. 529.

[9]George V. Wigram, *The Analytical Greek Lexicon of the New Testament* (Peabody, MA: Hendrickson Publishers, 1983), p. 273.

[10]Frederick Carl Eiselen, Edwin Lewis, and David G. Downey, *The Abingdon Bible Commentary* (New York: Abingdon Press, 1929), p. 1249.

[11]J. B. Lightfoot, *Saint Paul's Epistle to the Philippians* (Grand Rapids: Zondervan Publishing House, 1953), p. 164.

[12]*The New Jerusalem Bible* (New York: Doubleday, 1985), p. 1944.

[13]*The Amplified Bible* (Grand Rapids: Zondervan Bible Publishers, 1965), p. 309.

[14]J. E. Müeller, *The Epistle of Paul to the Philippians* (Grand Rapids: Wm. B. Eerdmans Publishing Company, 1988), p. 146.

[15]Lloyd John Ogilvie, *Let God Love You* (Waco: Word Books, 1974), p. 153.

[16]Joseph Henry Thayer, *A Greek-English Lexicon of the New Testament* (Grand Rapids: Baker Book House, 1977), p. 419.

[17]Richard Francis Weymouth, *The New Testament in Modern Speech* (Boston: The Pilgrim Press, 1939), p. 469.

[18]James Moffatt, *A New Translation of the Bible* (New York: Harper & Brothers Publishing, 1935), p. 250.

Chapter 6

[1]William Glasser, M.D., *Reality Therapy* (New York: Harper & Row, 1965), p. 29.

[2]*One Day at a Time in Al-Anon* (New York: Al-Anon Family Group Headquarters, Inc., 1972), p. 376.

[3]William Glasser, M.D., *Reality Therapy* (New York: Harper & Row, 1965).

[4]Eric Berne, M.D., *Games People Play: The Basic Handbook of Transactional Analysis* (New York: Ballantine Books, 1964).

[5]Thomas A. Harris, *I'm OK — You're OK* (New York: Harper & Row, 1967).

[6]Viktor E. Frankl, *Man's Search for Meaning* (New York: Washington Square Press, 1963).

[7]A. Ellis, *Reason and Emotion in Psychotherapy* (New York: Lyle Stuart, 1962).

[8]Jean Piaget, *Adoption and Intelligence: Organic Selection and Phenocopy* (Chicago: University of Chicago Press, 1980).

[9]Abraham H. Maslow, *Toward a Psychology of Being* (New York: Van Nostrand Reinhold, 1962), Chapter 2.

[10]Herbert A. Otto, *Human Potentialities* (St. Louis: Warren H. Green, 1968).

[11]James V. McConnell, *Understanding Human Behavior* (New York: Holt, Rinehart and Winston, 1974).

[12]D. Martyn-Lloyd Jones, *Spiritual Depression: Its Causes and Cure* (Grand Rapids: Wm. B. Eerdmans, 1965).

[13]Pierre Teilhard de Chardin, *The Divine Milieu* (New York: Harper & Row, 1960).

[14]Paul Tournier, *The Meaning of Persons* (New York: Harper & Row, 1957).

[15]J. Wesley Bready, *This Freedom — Whence?* (New York: American Tract Society, 1946).

[16]Thomas E. Gaddis, *Birdman of Alcatraz* (New Orleans: River City Press, 1955).

[17]Corrie ten Boom, *The Hiding Place* (Washington Depot, CN: Chosen Books, distributed by Fleming H. Revell, 1971).

Chapter 7

[1]Samuel M. Shoemaker, *How You Can Find Happiness*, quoted in: Frank S. Mead *Twelve Thousand Religious Quotations* (Grand Rapids: Baker Book House, 1989), p. 210.

Chapter 8

[1]Sigmund Freud, M.D., LL.D., *The General Introduction to Psychoanalysis* (Garden City, NY: Permabooks, 1935).

[2]Erich Fromm, *Escape From Freedom* (New York: Avon, 1941).

[3]Leonard E. Read (ed.), *Essays on Liberty*, Volume II (New York: The Foundation for Economic Education, Inc., 1954).

[4]Alcoholics Anonymous World Services. Inc., *Twelve Steps and Twelve Traditions* (New York: A.A. Grapevine, Inc., 1953), especially Step 10.

Chapter 9

[1]William C. Lantz, Jr., Ph.D., *The Unearned Relationship: Relationship Therapy* (unpublished manuscript).

BIBLIOGRAPHY

Alcoholics Anonymous World Services. Inc. *Twelve Steps and Twelve Traditions*. New York: A.A. Grapevine, Inc., 1953.

Aristotle, *Rhetoric* (in *The Great Books*, translated by W. Rhys Roberts). Chicago: Encyclopedia Britannica, 1990.

Barclay, William. *The Letters to the Philippians, Colossians and Thessalonians* (one volume of *The Daily Study Bible*). Philadelphia: The Westminster Press, 1959.

Bauer, Walter. *A Greek-English Lexicon of the New Testament*, Second Edition. Chicago: University of Chicago Press, 1979.

Berne, Eric, M.D. *Games People Play: The Basic Handbook of Transactional Analysis*. New York: Ballantine Books, 1964.

Birk, Lee, M.D. *Biofeedback: Behavioral Medicine*. New York: Grune & Stratton, 1973.

Bready, J. Wesley. *This Freedom — Whence?* New York: American Tract Society, 1946.

Brown, Barbara B., Ph.D. *New Mind New Body: Biofeedback: New Directions for the Mind*. New York: Harper & Row, 1974.

Bryant, Al (compiler). *Storehouse of Poetry*. Grand Rapids: Zondervan Publishing House, 1979.

Coon, Dennis. *Introduction to Psychology: Exploration and Application*. St. Paul: West Publishing, 1977.

de Chardin, Pierre Teilhard. *The Divine Milieu*. New York: Harper & Row, 1960.

Dyer, Wayne W. *Your Erroneous Zones*. New York: Avon Books, 1976.

Eiselen, Frederick Carl; Lewis, Edwin; and Downey, David G. *The Abingdon Bible Commentary*. New York: Abingdon Press, 1982.

Ellis, A. *Reason and Emotion in Psychotherapy*. New York: Lyle Stuart, 1962.

Frankl, Viktor E. *Man's Search for Meaning*. New York: Washington Square Press, 1963.

Freud, Sigmund, M.D., LL.D. *A General Introduction to Psychoanalysis*. Garden City, NY: Permabooks, 1935.

Fromm, Erich. *Escape From Freedom*. New York: Avon, 1941.

Gaddis, Thomas A. *Birdman of Alcatraz*. New Orleans: River City Press, 1955.

Glasser, William, M.D. *Reality Therapy*. New York: Harper & Row, 1965.

Harris, Thomas A. *I'm OK — You're OK*. New York: Harper & Row, 1967.

Hawthorne, Gerald. *Word Biblical Commentary*, Volume 43. Waco: Word Books, 1982.

Holy Bible: New International Version. Grand Rapids: Zondervan Publishing House, 1973, 1978, 1984.

Jones, D. Martyn-Lloyd. *Spiritual Depression: Its Causes and Cure*. Grand Rapids: Wm. B. Eerdmans, 1965.

Lantz, William C., Jr., Ph.D. *Goal Therapy*. Unpublished manuscript.

Lantz, William C., Jr., Ph.D. *Influence Therapy*. Unpublished manuscript.

Lantz, William C., Jr., Ph.D., *The Unearned Relationship: Relationship Therapy*. Unpublished manuscript.

Lightfoot, J. B. *Saint Paul's Epistle to the Philippians*. Grand Rapids: Zondervan Publishing House, 1953.

Maslow, Abraham H. *Toward a Psychology of Being*. New York: Van Nostrand Reinhold, 1962.

McConnell, James V. *Understanding Human Behavior.* New York: Holt, Rinehart and Winston, 1974.

Mead, Frank S. *Twelve Thousand Religious Quotations.* Grand Rapids: Baker Book House, 1989.

Moffatt, James. *A New Translation of the Bible.* New York: Harper and Brothers Publishing, 1935.

Müller, J. E. *The Epistle of Paul to the Philippians.* Grand Rapids: Wm. B. Eerdmans Publishing Company, 1988.

Munn, Norman; Fernald, L. Dodge, Jr.; and Fernald, Peter. *Basic Psychology.* Boston: Houghton Mifflin, 1972.

Newman, James W. *Release Your Brakes!* Thorofare, NJ: Charles B. Slack, Inc., 1977.

Ogilvie, Lloyd John. *Let God Love You.* Waco: Word Books, 1974.

One Day at a Time in Al-Anon. New York: Al-Anon Family Group Headquarters, Inc., 1972.

Otto, Herbert A. *Human Potentialities.* St. Louis: Warren H. Green, 1968.

Piaget, Jean. *Adoption and Intelligence: Organic Selection and Phenocopy.* Chicago: University of Chicago Press, 1980.

Read, Leonard E. (ed.). *Essays on Liberty,* Volume II. New York: The Foundation for Economic Education, Inc., 1954.

Schaeffer, Francis. *A Christian Manifesto.* Westchester, IL: Crossway Books, 1984.

Shoemaker, Samuel M. *How You Can Find Happiness.* Quoted in: Mead, Frank S. *Twelve Thousand Religious Quotations.* Grand Rapids: Baker Book House, 1989.

Stern, Alfred. *Sartre.* New York: Dell Publishing Company, 1967.

ten Boom, Corrie. *The Hiding Place.* Washington Depot, CN: Chosen Books, distributed by Fleming H. Revell, 1971.

Thayer, Joseph Henry. *A Greek-English Lexicon of the New Testament*. Grand Rapids: Baker Book House, 1977.

The Amplified Bible. Grand Rapids: Zondervan Bible Publishers, 1965.

The Great Books. Chicago: Encyclopedia Britannica, 1990.

The Living Bible. Wheaton, IL: Tyndale House Publishers, 1971.

The New Jerusalem Bible. New York: Doubleday, 1985.

The New King James Version. Nashville: Thomas Nelson, Inc., 1979, 1980, 1982, 1984.

The Revised Standard Version of the Bible. New York: National Council of the Churches of Christ in the United States of America, 1946, 1952, 1971, 1973.

Tournier, Paul. *The Meaning of Persons*. New York: Harper & Row, 1957.

Tweedie, Donald F., Jr. *Logotherapy and the Christian Faith*. Grand Rapids: Baker Book House, 1961.

Ungersma, A. J. *The Search for Meaning*. Philadelphia: The Westminster Press, MCMLXI.

Watson, J. B. *Behaviorism*. Rev. Ed. Chicago: University of Chicago Press, 1958.

Weymouth, Richard Francis. *The New Testament in Modern Speech*. Boston: The Pilgrim Press, 1939.

Wicks, Robert R. *The Interpreter's Bible* (Volume XI, Exposition of Philippians). New York: Abingdon Press, 1955.

Wigram, George V. *The Analytical Greek Lexicon of the New Testament*. Peabody, MA: Hendrickson Publishers, 1983.

Wilcox, Ella Wheeler. "The Winds of Fate." Quoted in: Bryant, Al (compiler). *Storehouse of Poetry*. Grand Rapids: Zondervan Publishing House, 1979.

ABOUT THE AUTHORS

William C. ("Bill") Lantz, Jr., received a B.S. degree from Northwestern University and a M.A. degree from the University of Denver. He was awarded eight scholarships and fellowships during the course of his formal education which was capped by a Ph.D. degree from the University of Southern California. His major area of study was neurolinguistics, a form of psychotherapy. He also attended Fuller Seminary and is now an ordained minister.

Dr. Lantz has taught at the University of Southern California, the University of Denver, Pasadena College and Oral Roberts University. He was formerly a full professor at Fuller Seminary, where he taught for ten years. He was Director of Consultation and Education at Tulsa Psychiatric Center for seven years. Since 1977 he has been the director of Heritage Services, a counseling and training agency located in Tulsa. He also serves part time as Minister of Healing/ Counseling at First United Methodist Church of Tulsa.

For years Dr. Lantz taught classes in leadership, human relations, communication and personal development for companies and organizations such as General Motors, North American Rockwell, McDonnell Douglas, IBM, Dean Witter, Dale Carnegie, U.S. Jaycees, Ampex, Sales and Marketing Executives, Multilist, YMCA, Blue Cross-Blue Shield and various other commercial, religious, educational and civic groups. He has trained many thousands of business executives, ministers, teachers, counselors and other professionals to explore and utilize more of their skills and experience, spontaneously and effectively.

In addition to his training programs for individuals, companies, churches and community groups, Dr. Lantz is known for his writings, private counseling services and speeches.

Connie Lantz joins her husband in a unique ministry, counseling and teaching together as a team both at Heritage Services and First United Methodist Church in Tulsa, Oklahoma. Their counselees and trainees are referred to them by ministers, doctors, lawyers, former counselees, students, and others. Those they counsel and train appreciate the tremendous help and wisdom they receive from a Christian married couple who are also professionals.

At First United Methodist Church, Connie counsels members of the church and for the last ten years has been the coordinator of the Paraprofessional Counselors of the church. She supervises and trains members in lay counseling. At present, sixty members are actively counseling under her leadership. She also leads therapy groups and trains and supervises leaders for other therapy groups.

Connie and Bill have six children and nine grandchildren. Tulsa has been home for both of them since childhood.

What Is Your Decision?

If you have never received Jesus Christ as your personal Lord and Savior, why not do it right now? Simply repeat this prayer with sincerity: "Lord Jesus, I believe that You are the Son of God. I believe that You became man and died on the cross for my sins. I believe that God raised You from the dead and made You the Savior of the world. I confess that I am a sinner and I ask You to forgive me, and to cleanse me of all my sins. I accept Your forgiveness, and I receive You as my Lord and Savior. In Jesus' name, I pray. Amen."

> "...if you confess with your mouth, 'Jesus is Lord,' and believe in your heart that God raised him from the dead, you will be saved. For it is with your heart that you believe and are justified, and it is with your mouth that you confess and are saved....for, 'Everyone who calls on the name of the Lord will be saved.'"
>
> **Romans 10:9,10,13 NIV**
>
> "If we confess our sins, he is faithful and just and will forgive us our sins and purify us from all unrighteousness."
>
> **1 John 1:9 NIV**

Now that you have accepted Jesus as your Savior:

1. Read your Bible *daily* — it is your spiritual food that will make you a strong Christian.

2. Pray and talk to God daily — He desires for the two of you to communicate and share your lives with each other.

3. Share your faith with others. Be bold to let others know that Jesus loves them.

4. Regularly attend a local church where Jesus is preached, where you can serve Him and where you can fellowship with other believers.

5. Let His love in your heart touch the lives of others by your good works done in His name.

Please let us know of the decision you made. Write:

Honor Books
P.O. 55388
Tulsa, OK 74155